JOHN ALE⁤ ⁤LSON

Mansions
of Paris

Mansions of Paris

OLIVIER BLANC
JOACHIM BONNEMAISON

| Cover illustration
HÔTEL DE BRINVILLIERS
| Stairwell with
| 'French-style' paving.

| Page 2
HÔTEL DE NOIRMOUTIER
| The entrance, opening
| onto the main courtyard.

English Translation: Murray Wyllie
Editor: Jean-Claude Dubost
Editorial Assistants: Geneviève Meunier, Hélène Roquejoffre and Claire Néollier
Editorial Co-ordination: Erik Boursier
Editorial Aide: Ann Sautier-Greening and Béatrice Weité
Cover Design: Laurent Gudin
Graphic Design: Véronique Rossi
Photographic Assistant: Sonia Duclos
Typesetting and Filmsetting: DV Arts Graphiques, Chartres
Photoengraving: Litho Service T. Zamboni, Verona

© FINEST SA / PIERRE TERRAIL EDITIONS, PARIS 1998
The Art Book Subsidiary of BAYARD PRESSE SA
English edition: © 1998
Publisher's n°: 216
ISBN 2-87939-180-6
Printed in Italy

HÔTEL CARNAVALET
The grand staircase: *trompe-l'œil*
perspective painted in 1748
by the Brunettis, elder
and younger, originally in Hôtel
de Luynes, Rue Saint-Dominique,
which has now been demolished.

Page 6 |
HÔTEL DE BOURRIENNE
Detail of a painted door
in the bedchamber.

CONTENTS

INTRODUCTION

HÔTEL DE SEIGNELAY
Façade overlooking
the garden, built in 1715
by Germain Boffrand.

The Parisian *hôtels particuliers* are a rich legacy from a refined by-gone age. The French expression *hôtel particulier* refers to a type of residence comparable to the Roman palazzo or the Palladian villa. The English equivalent is known as a 'mansion' or 'town house', depending on size, and – as for instance, Marble Hill House, Ranger's House or Chiswick House near London – bears the name of either the geographical location or the former owner. Nowadays, the French term is applied to a wide range of buildings, including large palaces – such as Hôtel de Salm or Hôtel de Soubise– the small Parliament House in the Marais district, the vast aristocratic mansions in Place Vendôme, 'follies' nestling in greenery like the Carré de Baudoin in Rue Ménilmontant, or 'smaller', but no less elegant houses like that in Rue de La Rochefoucauld designed by the architect Rousseau.

The charm of a city like Paris, fashioned by two millennia of art and history, resides above all in these mansions which were built at different periods, subject to the vagaries of royal or aristocratic fashion, the growth of trade, or the burgeoning influence of the bourgeoisie. At various times, the king lived in the Île de la Cité, the Bastille, Hôtel Saint-Pol, Les Tournelles, the Louvre and the Tuileries, and on each occasion courtiers built their own residences in the vicinity of the royal palace. Nowadays, the majority of these aristocratic residences have vanished, notably the mansions which once stood on the sites presently occupied by the Louvre pyramid and Place du Carrousel. There remain, however, two unique ensembles which characterize the domestic architecture of the Ancien Régime: the mansions in the Marais, mostly dating from the 17th century, and those which stand in the Faubourg Saint-Germain. In addition, a few essentially Neo-Classical buildings have survived in the 9th arrondissement of the city. These historic mansions have been the subject of numerous books and learned articles; thanks to old notarial deeds, architectural plans, and engravings, the state of such residences in their prime is relatively well-documented.

Various factors influenced the choice of the aristocratic clients who commissioned such mansions: the degree of status they were seeking to proclaim, their wealth, rank, or level of aesthetic taste.

Since the mid-16th century, members of the wealthy classes had vied with each other to acquire stately homes with luxurious interiors. The greatest artists were recruited to design, build and embellish these residences which invariably included a custom-designed garden. Architects such as Mansart, Courtonne, Delamair, Gabriel, Brongniart and Bélanger drew up the plans; interiors were provided by designers such as Boffrand, Boiston, and Lelièvre; and, finally, leading royal artists (Coypel, Watteau, Boucher, Ondry) contributed elegant ornamental panels, overdoors and pier paintings. Decorators also played a key role in matching the interior architecture of the private rooms – stucco decors and panelling – with the furnishings, particulary in the bedchambers. When Marie de Médicis had the highly-praised Luxembourg Palace built in Paris, French influence in the entire field of decorative arts swept through the aristocratic houses of Europe, supplanting the previous Italian model until the French Revolution. In the 16th, 17th and 18th centuries, the heyday of the 'old mansions' of Paris, every member of the legal, financial or hereditary aristocracies felt duty-bound to acquire an attractive, luxurious residence. Some, moreover, were quite prepared to sacrifice function to aesthetic form, commissioning vast reception rooms and stately bedchambers, and attaching only minor importance to more convenient – and heatable – layouts. They were not, however, totally averse to comfort, and at every period, wealthy owners introduced new heating, lighting and plumbing techniques, not to mention improvements to what were described in contemporary notarial inventories as 'English-style' facilities...

Reception or state rooms were laid out on the ground floor, while the living quarters, normally separate apartments for husband and wife, occupied the first floor. There were, however, exceptions and in some instances the master bedchambers extended directly from the formal reception area. Other less ostentatious apartments were laid out in the wings or minor rooms on the upper floors to accommodate children and senior household staff. The ordinary servants lived in the attics, above the stables, or in tiny – sometimes windowless – bedrooms.

To the modern mind, perhaps the most striking aspect is the abundance of – admittedly cheaply available – servants. In the days before the advent of domestic appliances they carried out all the chores of

Jean-François de Troy
THE LUNCH OF OYSTERS
1735, oil on canvas,
180 × 126 cm (70 7/8 × 49 5/8 in).
Musée Condé, Chantilly.

Pages 14 and 15
THE ÉLYSÉE PALACE
Panelled reception room,
18th century.
Successively owned
by the Comte d'Évreux,
Madame de Pompadour
and Nicolas Beaujon,
the Élysée Palace is now the official residence of the President
of the French Republic.

| Michel-Barthélemy Ollivier
**ENGLISH TEA BEING SERVED
IN THE 'SALON DES QUATRE GLACES'
IN THE TEMPLE PALACE IN MAY 1766**
| 1776, oil on canvas,
68 × 53 cm (26 ³/₄ × 20 ⁷/₈ in).
Musée national du château, Versailles.

HÔTEL DE BOURBON-CONDÉ
Detail of the ceiling
in the oval reception room.
This mansion, a masterpiece
designed by the architect Brongniart
for Mlle de Bourbon-Condé,
was completed in 1786.

cleaning, upkeep, tidying and repairing, working in the kitchens – where meals were seldom prepared for fewer than ten people – or in the coach houses and stables where the horses were groomed and harnesses maintained, and in the carefully-tended gardens with their box hedges, ornamental orange trees and arbours or groves.

Above all, however, the aristocratic mansion or town house was intended as a glittering showcase where guests were received and, on occasion, high-ranking visitors shown around. Receptions, ranging from simple, and extremely popular, musical evenings to spectacular masked balls, were held regularly from autumn through to spring; and it was not uncommon for the mistress of the house to devote one day of the week to her 'at home'.

The history of the Parisian mansion is intimately intertwined with that of another 17th and 18th-century institution, the salon. These social gatherings, with their blend of ease, refinement and wit, were, in some cases, avant-garde forums for philosophy, literature and the arts. Somewhat hidebound and artificial in the early 17th century – as, for instance, the salons in the Hôtel de Rambouillet where society gossip substituted for wit – they opened up to the outside world

| Jean-François Bosio
LA BOUILLOTTE
AN OLD FRENCH CARD-GAME
C. 1804, etching,
34 × 49 cm (13 $^{7}/_{8}$ × 19 $^{1}/_{4}$ in).
Bibliothèque nationale de France,
cabinet des estampes, Paris.

François Dequevauviller,
after Lavreince |
THE CONCERT AUDIENCE
1784, etching,
32 × 46 cm (12 $^{7}/_{8}$ × 18 in).
Bibliothèque nationale de France,
cabinet des estampes, Paris.

and, by the eve of the Revolution, had become the hub of intellectual life. Besides concerts and balls, enlivened by illuminated displays and fireworks in the mansions' gardens, gambling was all the rage in elegant Parisian society. Every mansion boasted gaming-tables for its guests. The more persistently successive governments sought – in vain – to control or to ban gambling, the more the fashion thrived. When a group of Palais Royal gaming-house owners were heavily penalized, the passion for gambling reached fever pitch in the stately mansions of the Marquis de Genlis and the Marquis de Livry, in foreign embassies – such as those of Venice and Sweden – and, ultimately, at Versailles where, in the 1780s, the Comte d'Artois or the Duchesse de Polignac staked astronomical sums at the queen's gaming-table, to which every courtier dreamed of being invited.

Whether in Paris or in Versailles, women invariably played a central role in society gatherings and entertainments. It was they, in general, who stamped their personalities on the salons: rather exclusive and formal in some cases, relaxed and tolerant in others, and even occasionally – more often than is imagined – decidedly libertine.

Our brief selection of historic Parisian mansions – some well known, others less so – has provided a guiding theme allowing us to conjure up the memory of the great "Parisiennes" of the 17th and 18th centuries, whether they were women of sparkling wit and intelligence, like Mme de Sévigné and Mme Du Châtelet, amorous, like Mme Aubert de Fontenay, the Princesse de Charolais and Mlle O'Morphy, or scheming, like the Comtesse de Lamotte and the Marquise de Brinvilliers. Rather than offering a detailed description of the architectural masterpieces which these old mansions represent,

Nicolas de Larmessin,
after Lancret
MORNING
**"On relinquishing Morpheus'
sweet embrace..."**
1741, etching and dry-point,
28 × 37 cm (11 × 14 ⅝ in).
Bibliothèque nationale de France,
cabinet des estampes, Paris.

Louis Surugue, after Pater
THE JOY OF SUMMER
1744, etching and dry-point,
32 × 36 cm (12 ⅝ × 14 ⅛ in).
Bibliothèque nationale de France,
cabinet des estampes, Paris.

the aim of this book has been to bring to life the memories which are associated with them, to capture the fleeting ghosts of their former occupants, those charming women who were accomplished society hostesses, who loved culture, wit... or love itself. In short, perhaps for a last time to give substance to what has long been no more than a theatre of shadows.

Grand or unassuming, each of these noble mansions is imbued with a history which has become one with that of their former occupants, the men and women who have stamped these old buildings with something of their own personality. Confronted by our enquiring gaze, however, the venerable façades, the cracked steps of the stone staircases and the tarnished mirrors in the stately reception rooms, silent surviving witnesses to countless love affairs, dramas and intrigues, remain forever mute. In the present book we have endeavoured to venture beyond outward appearances, to attempt for a brief instant to light up the vanished interiors and to resurrect the long lost features and private lives of the hosts and hostesses of these stately houses which brim with forgotten secrets.

HÔTEL CARNAVALET

Decorative paintings featuring an animal motif – a collective work by Boucher, Fragonard and Huet (c. 1765). Today, these works constitute the decor of one of the rooms in the Musée Carnavalet.

1. The Marais

.de.Sully.

A Flamboyant Superintendent of Finances

Hôtel de Sully

62 Rue Saint-Antoine

| French School
THE DUC DE SULLY
| Early 17th century,
oil on wood, 57 × 42 cm
(22 ³/₈ × 16 ½ in).
| Musée Condé, Chantilly.

Hôtel de Sully takes its name from Maximilien de Béthune, Duc de Sully, Henri IV's chief minister. Sully is traditionally portrayed as methodical and serious, in contrast to his easy-going, fun-loving friend the king. Yet contemporary accounts paint a rather different picture from the subsequent legend, concocted in the 19th century. According to the former, M. and Mme de Sully often caused eyebrows to be raised in the Marais district.

Their famous mansion, a magnet for countless visitors, was built not far from Place Royale (known as Place des Vosges since the Revolution) which was laid out in 1605 on the site of the former royal palace, Les Tournelles. Work began in 1625, on a plot of land won at the gaming-tables by the financial speculator and banker M. de Mesme-Gallet. The designs are attributed to the great architect Jean Androuet du Cerceau. The lavish decoration and, in particular, the

THE WEST FAÇADE OVERLOOKING
THE COURTYARD
Allegorical bas-reliefs
representing the elements;
shown here, *Earth* and *Fire*.

type of staircase chosen, were inspired by architectural models considered outmoded in a period which marked the heyday of the more
restrained Louis XIII style. The façades and courtyards of the town
houses on Place des Vosges are typical of the latter. Nevertheless, Hôtel
de Sully, 'standing between courtyard and garden', and provided with
an orangery, remains one of the finest examples of domestic architecture in the reign of Louis XIII. Moreover, it displays several affinities
with the rather less well-conserved Hôtel de Mayenne which stands
opposite at 21 Rue Saint-Antoine.

When, in 1634, the counsellor to 'good King Henri' was promoted
from Grand Master of Artillery to the highest office in the kingdom,
he left his official residence in the Arsenal and moved into M. de
Mesme-Gallet's brand new mansion. The precise layout and decoration of the premises as they existed when Sully took up residence with
his second wife, Rachel de Cochefilet, have come down to us from
detailed inventories. Today, a few vestiges of former splendour remain,
such as the painted beams in the large ground-floor reception room,
the coffered entrance vault with its decorative ceiling roses, and the
monumental staircase. To the right of this staircase, on the ground
floor, lay the duchess's apartment, furnished with "six white satin
tapestries embellished with embroidery" and a bed "the cover of which
was decorated with silver and gold trimmings". The lady, known then
as Mme de Rosny, from the name of the Sully domains along the
Seine valley, was the daughter of a Parisian lawyer who had converted
to Protestantism. The couple were held in great esteem at court, as
witnessed by Henri IV's declaration on the birth of the duchess's third
son: "I wish that God would grant her twelve a year, for it would be
a pity if such fine stock produced no offshoots." Sully – whom the
king considered an excellent Superintendent of Finances – reaped
enormous advantages from his influential office. Not to be outdone,
Mme de Sully, who was no beauty, used her worldly wisdom to
achieve her own ends. For instance, she obtained a life annuity of
thirty thousand *livres* from the royal coffers for M. de Schomberg,

Pages 28 and 29 |
THE MAIN COURTYARD SEEN FROM
THE TERRACE OVERLOOKING THE STREET
Hôtel de Sully remains one
of the finest examples of domestic
architecture during the reign
of Louis XIII (1610-1643).

PASSAGEWAY LINKING
THE COURTYARD AND GARDEN
| The ceiling is in carved stone.

THE LARGE GROUND-FLOOR ROOM
The ceiling with its painted joists
dates from the 17th century. |

with whom she was infatuated. Hugues de l'Estoile relates that "a charming painting of Adam and Eve representing M. and Mme de Sully nude" was circulating in Paris. "The tree of life", he writes, "was naively depicted, with a snake twined around the trunk offering a purse to Mme de Sully, while above, between the lady and her husband, appeared President Duret who, with outstretched neck and arms, was kissing the lady on the mouth".

Shortly before Henri IV's assassination, the Duc de Sully fell from grace and, according to Richelieu, the king even "considered relieving him of the control of finances". After a while, Sully solemnly resigned his post, accepting one hundred thousand crowns as indemnity. When, on their way back home to the château at Rosny, Rachel de Cochefilet upbraided her husband for his 'haughtiness' and 'pride', he angrily retorted that "he had made a duchess of the daughter of

Pages 30 and 31

THE ORANGERY, ALSO KNOWN AS THE 'PETIT SULLY'

Standing at the foot of the garden facing due south and adjacent to the neighbouring Hôtel de Chaulnes, it was built between 1634 and 1641.

THE GARDEN FAÇADE

This façade echoes the courtyard façade.

a solicitous little quibbler". The couple grew estranged. When, both already elderly, they finally settled in their new mansion in Rue Saint-Antoine, they did not go unnoticed. Sully would don the most extravagant hats and dance the pavane with the ladies of ill-repute procured for him by his former secretaries. On other occasions, the former Superintendent of Finances would be seen strolling beneath the arcades in Place Royale, decked out in old-fashioned gold chains and diamond insignia. "Nothing pleased him more", writes the scholar Lefeuve, "than to be taken for the most foul-mouthed lord in the world. Besides, he couldn't care less about his wife's infidelities..."

Prince de Henrichemont, the second Duc de Sully, moved into the premises on the death of his father in 1641; the layout and painted and sculpted decoration as they exist today were, in fact, largely inspired by his wife, Charlotte Séguier. Less frivolous than her mother-

in-law, she was well received in the Place des Vosges literary salons. After four generations of Sullys, the mansion was occupied by high-ranking aristocratic families such as the Turgots de Saint-Clair (1752-1771) and the Boisgelins (1771-1796). It was spared the ravages of later speculators – for whom, moreover, the Marais, which had eventually become a working-class district, held little appeal – and the 'commercial vandalism' of the 19th and early 20th centuries, before finally being purchased by the state in 1944. Today, admirably restored, it houses the headquarters of the Caisse nationale des monuments historiques (the French National Historic Buildings Commission).

THE FAÇADE OVERLOOKING THE COURTYARD
An exterior flight of steps, or perron, embellished with two ornamental female sphinxes, leads to the main building.

A Survivor of the Terror

Hôtel Mégret de Sérilly

106 Rue Vieille-du-Temple

**VIEW OF THE CENTRAL COURTYARD
FROM THE MAIN BUILDING**
This Louis XIII mansion
has a pink brickwork façade.

This relatively little-known mansion, designed by Jean Thiriot, architect to Louis XIII, was one of the most palatial residences in the Marais. It had extensive gardens, a courtyard faced with pink brickwork – which has survived virtually intact in its original condition – and sumptuous interior decorations, renovated or created by leading 17th-century artists who had been commissioned by the financier Mégret de Sérilly to impress his wife Marie-Anne. The latter's story started out as a fairy tale only to end in tragedy.

The mansion had been built on land belonging to the d'Épernon family. This family was still extremely influential in the early 17th century and one of their town houses – now a school – still stands not far away, between Hôtel Salé and Hôtel de Sérilly itself, which was formerly known as Hôtel Mallebranche, and later Hôtel du Tillet, from the names of its successive owners.

In 1765, the vast building had been auctioned off by the heirs of Comtesse Desvieux to Jean-Baptiste Thomas, Marquis de Pange, bailiff of the city of Metz. In 1776, Thomas sold the house and gardens to his son-in-law, Antoine-Jean-François Mégret de Sérilly, Treasurer-General Extraordinary for War, who had used his lucrative office to amass great wealth. He spared no pains to please his new wife, Marie-Anne Thomas de Pange de Dommangeville, an ash-blonde beauty with grey-blue eyes who had many suitors, including the Chevalier de Pange, her cousin, and the poet André Chenier, introduced to the attractive young girl at the family residence, Château de Mareuil, while still an adolescent. To impress his betrothed, Sérilly commissioned expensive renovation work on the mansion in the 'Vieille Rue du Temple'.

Life at the mansion in the early 1780s was a dazzling, never-ending round of revelry, accompanied by illuminated displays amidst the flowers blooming in the magnificent, newly-replanted gardens. During the summer months, the couple moved to the Mégret de Sérilly family seat – a château lavishly renovated and redecorated by Brongniart and Chevotet at enormous cost – at Passy, near Sens. Then, suddenly, catastrophe struck: Mégret de Sérilly was forced into liquidation and declared bankrupt. His financial downfall caused a great stir and he was forced to resign from his post as treasurer. Fortunately, Mme Thomas de Pange, Sérilly's mother-in-law, made over to him a town house in Rue des Capucines. He sold it to his creditors who received immediate compensation. But the couple had to tighten their belts and bid farewell to their extravagant style of life. In 1789, Mme de Sérilly, granted a temporary respite from other creditors, despite the large sums which her husband still owed the state, whiled away the long hours in a ground-floor boudoir in the right wing of her Marais mansion. This boudoir, with its tall windows opening onto the gardens which were screened from Rue de Thorigny by a row of trees, contains a striking white marble fireplace sculpted by Clodion. The arabesque panels in

THE COURTYARD FAÇADE

Work on the mansion began in 1620 to plans by Thiriot and the building was extended in 1686.

the room were decorated by Rousseau de La Rottière, the paintings are by Natoire and the ceiling decoration, representing Jupiter on his Olympian throne, is the work of Lagrenée. The decoration of this architectural gem (nowadays re-assembled in the Victoria and Albert Museum in London) involved four of the greatest 17th-century artists, not to mention Houdon, who executed a portrait bust of the mistress of the house which may formerly have stood on the mantelpiece.

This bust, now in the Wallace Collection in London, shows the young woman in a solemn, contemplative mood, apparently sensing the tribulations that lay in store for her. Elsewhere, and notably in the large reception room, carved and gilded wood panelling by Ledoux and sculptures by Roland formed a majestic ensemble, part of which is now in the United States.

Rather than emigrate, the Sérillys divided their time between Paris and the country, thus avoiding harassment up until the Terror when the Committee of General Safety issued a warrant for the arrest of the former Treasurer of War along with his brother, M. Mégret d'Étigny, their relative and lady of the neighbouring château – the widow of the Minister Montmorin who had perished during the September Massacres in

Jean-Antoine Houdon |
MARIE-ANNE THOMAS DE PANGE,
MARQUISE MÉGRET DE SÉRILLY
1782, marble, height 62 cm (24 3/8 in).
The Wallace Collection, London.

1792 – and her children. Following rash attempts in Paris to obtain her husband's freedom, Mme de Sérilly was herself arrested and indicted in a joint accusation. When, together with Madame Élisabeth, Louis XVI's sister, and twenty-three other companions in misfortune, she heard the court announce the sentence of death by guillotine, she fainted. Mme de Montmorin, also condemned to death, stepped forward and requested to speak, pointing out that Mme de Sérilly was pregnant. By order of the judges, the latter was separated from the other unfortunates who were hustled out to waiting tumbrels in the courtyard of the Palais de Justice. Saved by a miracle, Mme de Sérilly was nevertheless subsequently declared dead, her death certificate having being drawn up at the same time as those of the other victims condemned on 10 May (21 Floréal in the Revolutionary calendar). This error was not put right until she was set free following the fall of Robespierre on 9 Thermidor. Summoned as a witness at the trial of Fouquier-Tinville, she appeared in court clutching her death certificate. The effect created was that of a spectre returning from beyond the grave to testify in the name of the victims against the public prosecutor and judges who now, in turn, found themselves in the dock. Concerning her husband's arrest at the Château de Passy, she told the court of the exactions perpetrated by the Committee of General Safety agents, "so disgusting that they would not have behaved differently in a town taken by storm".

Mme de Sérilly was re-married in 1795 to her cousin the Chevalier de Pange, André Chénier's friend. Widowed once again, she then married the Marquis de Montesquiou Fezensac. Dufort de Cheverny, who saw her briefly in April 1797, relates that she looked unchanged, despite all the misfortunes that had befallen her and her five pregnancies: "She was every bit as beautiful as when I'd seen her last". She was living in a dingy apartment in Rue Chabanais in surroundings utterly different from her luxurious mansion in Rue Vieille-du-Temple which had been confiscated as state property in 1792 and put up for sale the following year. After a succession of different owners, the mansion was rented to the scholar Rousselin de Saint-Albin, trustee of the Barras papers, who bought it in 1846. Although his heirs still owned the property at the beginning of the present century, they had already begun to sell off the magnificent original decors.

Nowadays, the gardens have been largely encroached upon by little red buildings, erected with utter disregard for the elegant classical architecture standing opposite.

DETAIL OF THE FAÇADE OVERLOOKING THE COURTYARD
Brick facing is a common early-17th-century feature.

A Martyr in the Cause of Liberty

Hôtel Le Peletier de Saint-Fargeau

29 Rue de Sévigné

THE GRAND STAIRCASE
Designed with an extreme purity
of line, the staircase leads
to the collections in the City
of Paris Historical Museum
(Musée Carnavalet).

The site on which Hôtel Le Peletier de Saint-Fargeau stands was formerly marshland covering the north-eastern area of the city within the walls built by King Philip II Augustus. In the late Middle Ages, the friars from the Priory of Sainte-Catherine-du-Val-des-Escholiers drained the marshes and reclaimed the land for cultivation – hence the Old French designation *coutures* (arable land) from which, in turn, Rue de la Culture-Sainte-Catherine (present-day Rue de Sévigné) derived its name. In 1545 a first residence was built by Michel de Champrond. By 1686, the original house was in a terrible state of dilapidation when Michel Le Peletier, Lord of Souzy, decided to have it completely rebuilt, commissioning the architect Pierre Bullet to supervise the work. Although it has retained its fine exterior, only one of the 17th-century rooms – redecorated under Louis XVI, when large mirrors surmounted by garlands and flanked by trophied pilasters were added – and a still impressive monumental staircase have survived. The mansion remained in the hands of the Le Peletier family of Parisian parliamentarians as it stands today, with its façades overlooking the courtyard and gardens and its orangery, until the Revolution. In 1793, the owners were the two Le Peletier half-brothers, Félix and Louis-Michel, who had been brought up in the family château at Saint-Fargeau near Auxerre. Louis-Michel Le Peletier de Saint-Fargeau, Advocate General and President of the Paris Parlement on the eve of the Revolution, was elected to the Estates General by the Paris nobility, and later to the Convention as representative for the Yonne department. Although moderate in word and deed, he nevertheless distanced himself from the majority of his own order during the debate on whether or not to declare war. He also supported the abolition of honorary titles voted by the Constituent Assembly of which he became President in May 1790. Finally, he drew up a report on the penal code in which he advocated the abolition of the death penalty.

During Louis XVI's trial, Michel Le Peletier came under pressure from some of his royalist friends, notably Regnaud de Saint-Jean d'Angely and André Chénier, assembled at Versailles together with the bankers

Le Couteulx, to use his influence among his colleagues in favour of the deposed monarch. However, having first argued that the king should be imprisoned, he then adopted a diametrically opposite stand and voted for the death sentence without appeal or reprieve. Some royalists were unable to forgive the high-ranking aristocrat and, on the very eve of the king's execution, a royal bodyguard by name of Pâris stabbed Le Peletier in the heart as he was sitting in a café in the Palais-Royal, his favourite haunt. The assassination caused a great political stir and Le Peletier was given a state funeral. He was officially declared a "martyr in the cause of liberty" and his bloodstained corpse was publicly exhibited on a pedestal in the centre of Place Vendôme before being buried with great pomp in the Panthéon, where Félix Le Peletier de Saint-Fargeau delivered a eulogy beside his elder brother's coffin, ending: "Like my brother, I vote for the death of tyrants". In 1780, Louis-Michel Le Peletier had married a young lady called Joly de Fleury and the couple had a daughter, Suzanne, whose features are familiar to

us from a portrait by David (who also immortalized her father's assassination and then, the following July, that of Marat). The family mansion was legally inherited by Suzanne Le Peletier following her marriage with her cousin Mortefontaine. Converted to intransigent royalism by her husband, she took part in the clandestine political meetings held at their home in Hôtel Poyanne in Rue du Faubourg-Saint-Honoré. In 1803 she sold the old house in Rue de la Culture-Sainte-Catherine, where six successive generations of Le Peletiers had lived, to a mechanic who had amassed a fortune during the Revolution.

In the course of the 19th century, Hôtel Le Peletier de Saint-Fargeau lost its former splendour. In 1897, the City of Paris bought the property and installed their Historical Library on the premises, putting an end to the lingering decline of the fine old building. The library was later moved to the neighbouring Hôtel Lamoignon and nowadays part of Hôtel Le Peletier is used to exhibit collections belonging to the Musée Carnavalet.

THE ORANGERY
Built between 1686 and 1689 by Bullet, the Orangery still stands as a wing giving onto the garden, elegant as ever.

FROM GUNPOWDER STORE TO NATIONAL LIBRARY

Pavillon de l'Arsenal

1 and 3 Rue de Sully

As it was extremely dangerous to manufacture and store gunpowder and munitions in the Louvre, King François I had ordered his Comptroller of Artillery to requisition two municipal barns which lay behind the Celestine convent on the eastern edge of Paris in order to provide an arsenal. But on 20 January 1563, this new royal arsenal was destroyed by a gigantic gunpowder explosion.

Charles IX had the arsenal rebuilt and enlarged into a vast quadrilateral standing along the banks of the small branch of the Seine opposite the Île Louviers (then still separated from the Right Bank), and extending from Rue du Petit-Musc to Boulevard Bourdon. The new buildings surrounded five interior courtyards and a residential mansion was provided for the Grand Master of Artillery. On the appointment of Maximilien de Béthune, Duc de Sully, a friend of Henri IV, to the latter post, the mansion was enlarged and embellished. Sully lived in the Arsenal from 1594 to 1610, gradually transforming the official residence into an attractive dwelling. Surrounded by a small entourage of friends, he held dazzling receptions and balls to which leading court figures were invited. Henri IV frequently called on his minister, and even expressed his wish to have personal accommodation provided there. Accordingly, a pavilion was built for the king, but Henri was assassinated before he could make use of it.

In 1634, Maréchal De La Mailleraye was placed in command of the Arsenal and took up official residence. "He is a great besieger of cities," Tallemant des Réaux informs us, "but has no time for campaign warfare. Although brave, he is an exceptionally violent braggart." De La Mailleraye was so brutal that "when he got angry with his wife, he used to thrash her with his marshal's baton". The Maréchale, Marie de

JEANNE
ESTHER

LA·PVCELLE·
·VER·XVI·CHAP·4

THE ORATORY

This room is adjacent to
Marie de Cossé-Brissac's
bedchamber.
The De La Mailleraye
family monogram is visible
on the wood panelling.

Cossé-Brissac, his second wife, was a sparkling wit. According to Mme de Motteville, her beauty lay in "her delicate features, extremely pleasant manner and attractive figure". She was also gifted with a very pretty voice. Cardinal de Retz, and then Cardinal de Richelieu, were both "swept off their feet" by such an abundance of graceful attributes. And it did not go unnoticed that, all of a sudden, the latter cardinal had found frequent business to attend to at the Arsenal where the lady he called his "dear cousin" happened to live. The Maréchale, however, vaunted her marital fidelity and, added Mme de Motteville, "oozed with self-styled virtue". Saint-Simon also maintained that the reason she wasn't more frequently unfaithful to her husband – whose origins she sneered at, claiming her own descent from the Caesars – was because she was too terrified of Hell. Nevertheless, no sooner had her husband died in the war in Ireland than she wed her bashful lover, Charles Chalmot de Saint-Ruth. However, Saint-Simon mischievously adds: "She remained careful not to forfeit her title of duchess by officially registering the marriage"!

Marie de Cossé-Brissac had Henri IV's former private study magnificently redecorated and converted into a bedchamber for herself. Whether the paintings in the bedroom were executed by Simon Vouet and his pupils, or by Claude Vignon, remains a matter for debate. Next to this fine room was an oratory decorated with wood panelling featuring the De La Mailleraye and Cossé-Brissac family monograms.

The occupants who succeeded Maréchal De La Mailleraye and his extravagant wife made no alterations to the Grand Master of Artillery's residence until the arrival of the Duc and Duchesse du Maine, who had the apartments partially redecorated by Boffrand in 1718. The duchess's salon still boasts its fine monochrome overdoors painted by Bouchardon and copied from the bas-reliefs on the Grenelle fountain. Before Mme de Genlis held her literary salon there in Napoleonic times, one of the apartments had been occupied in 1789 by the Prince de Montbarrey, the disgraced Minister of War. When, in July that year, rioters appeared seeking gunpowder and weapons to storm the Bastille, the prince was mistaken for the governor of that fortress, M. de Launay, and narrowly escaped his fate.

The most notable resident was Marc-Antoine-René Voyer de Paulmy, son of the Marquis d'Argenson who commanded the Arsenal under Louis XV and Louis XVI, by which time its importance had diminished. An erudite patron of the arts, for more than thirty-five years he devoted his leisure time to building up a library systematically from the

THE BEDCHAMBER
Formerly Sully's private study, it was redecorated by Simon Vouet (or Claude Vignon) in 1637 for Marie de Cossé-Brissac, Maréchale De La Mailleraye, who used it as her bedchamber.

nucleus of his father's own collection of books. The library soon acquired a wide reputation and Paulmy placed it at the disposal of men of letters and scholars. It grew even larger when he purchased the remarkable collection of old books which his friend the Duc de La Vallière had assembled in his town house in Rue du Bac. Shortly before his death, in 1785, the Marquis de Paulmy donated his library to the Comte d'Artois, Louis XVI's brother, who besides acquired many of the books belonging to the Prince de Soubise. When Artois emigrated, his library, which had meanwhile become state property, was opened to the public by a decree of 9 Floréal in the Year V (late April 1797). At the Restoration, the Comte d'Artois waived all claim to the books in the Arsenal collections and when he succeeded to the throne as Charles X he appointed Charles Nodier to the post of curator. Under Nodier's curatorship, the library exercised a formative influence on what might be called the 'hard core' of the Romantic school: Hugo, Sainte-Beuve, Lamartine, Vigny, Dumas, along with the many others who regularly frequented the great temple of knowledge which the Arsenal had become. In later years, from 1901 onwards, Régnier, Barrès and Pierre Loüys were in turn to pool their literary talents under the auspices of the librarian José Maria de Heredia.

In 1856, restoration and extension work was carried out: the façades were entirely renovated, and the new interior layout entailed the removal of the panelling from the finest rooms and the oratory. The poor lighting in the new rooms no doubt contributed to the conservation of the paintings...

The library, which ranks second in importance to the Bibliothèque nationale, has recently been transferred to more suitable premises. The books are now housed in the new National Library buildings at Bercy, while the archives of the Ministry of Foreign Affairs are due to be moved from the cramped facilities at the Quai d'Orsay and will replace the historic collections built up by such figures as d'Argenson, Soubise and La Vallière.

THE BEDCHAMBER CEILING

The allegorical composition, extolling
the virtues of the Maréchal's family,
features Apollo and the nine Muses
along with heraldic emblems.
The Renown of the Old World
and *The Renown of the New World*
are matched by *Glorious France*
and *Victory*.

An Exceptional Guest

Hôtel d'Albret

31 Rue des Francs-Bourgeois

THE FAÇADE OVERLOOKING THE STREET
The mansion was rebuilt
by the architect Vautrain
between 1740 and 1744.
The central bay features
an ornamental wrought-iron balcony.

A STAIRCASE
The square turned-wood
balusters date from 1638.

This dignified mansion takes its name from the Maréchal and Maréchale d'Albret, hosts to one of the most famous figures in French history, Françoise d'Aubigné, Marquise de Maintenon, who lived in the Marais for several years before being admitted to Louis XIV's court.

An initial residence was built in 1550 by Constable de Montmorency on the land belonging to the Priory of Sainte-Catherine. In 1586, this house was sold to Marie de Baudini. It subsequently changed hands several times before being restored in the early 17th century by Gabriel de Guénégaud for the dowry of his daughter Magdeleine on the latter's marriage to César-Phoébus d'Albret, Marshal of France. According to one biographer, d'Albret was a marshal "who would faint at the sight of a young wild boar". The wealthy, privileged couple had a sumptuous lifestyle and when they held receptions they were in the habit of calling on the help of friends. One such 'friend' was Françoise d'Aubigné, impoverished since the death of her husband, the burlesque poet Scarron. Although the d'Albrets made an outward show of respecting her, they never let slip any opportunity of humiliating her. Grudgingly admitted into the household as a 'servant' by her hosts, Mme Scarron developed an understandable repugnance for high society and its demeaning 'hospitality': "In the d'Albret and de Richelieu households", writes Saint-Simon, "Mme Scarron was treated as a mere dogsbody. She was expected to attend to every chore, to have wood fetched, to see if guests were soon to be served or whether this or that lady's or gentleman's coach had returned; to deal with countless errands long rendered unnecessary by the introduction of service bells."

The life of the future Marquise de Maintenon had been one of constant adventure since her birth in Niort prison. Her Protestant family had forfeited their privileges and had been ruined. While she was still a child, Richelieu had ordered the arrest of her father, himself the son of the great writer Agrippa d'Aubigné, along with his wife. Françoise followed her father to Martinique in the French West Indies whence she miraculously returned to France, a twelve-year-old orphan.

She was taken in by a cantankerous aunt from whose household she escaped by marrying the poet Scarron, already in ill-health and deformed, who settled for her sixteen-year-old beauty as dowry. The couple lived in the Marais district for eight years until Scarron's death in 1660. Reduced to impoverished circumstances, she offered her services to the Maréchale d'Albret who in return spared her no humiliation. During one reception, however, she caught the eye of the Marquis de Montespan who presented her to his charming young wife Athénaïs de Mortemart de Rochechouart. What followed is history: Françoise d'Aubigné, who, like her old friend Ninon de Lenclos lacked neither charm nor wit, obtained the singular privilege of being appointed governess to the illegitimate children of Louis XIV and Mme de Montespan who had become the king's acknowledged mistress. Within a few years, the king became captivated by Françoise d'Aubigné's patient manner, intelligence and sedate beauty, just at the point when he was beginning to tire of the flirtatious, scheming court ladies who fussed around him. From then on, Françoise d'Aubigné, now known as the Marquise de Maintenon, grew in the king's favour and was finally married morganatically to the monarch, with all the prerogatives of a Queen of France.

Meanwhile, the d'Albrets' only daughter – married to a cousin of the same name – had inherited the mansion where the Marquise, 'virtually queen', had suffered such smarting humiliation. In 1678, the daughter sold the mansion to M. Brunet de Chailly, Keeper of the Royal Treasury. The property then passed into the hands of the latter's nephew, President of the Paris Parlement; the President in turn bequeathed it to his son who was guillotined during the Revolution. The building, which still possessed its superb façade – one of the finest in the Marais –, was confiscated as state property and sold off.

Acquired by the Paris authorities, Hôtel d'Albret underwent extensive restoration work to the courtyard and façades, while the former interior layout was irretrievably impaired by the removal of the panelling and chimney pieces. Nowadays it accommodates the City of Paris Directorate for Cultural Affairs.

Pierre Mignard |
PORTRAIT OF FRANÇOISE D'AUBIGNÉ, MARQUISE DE MAINTENON
C. 1694, oil on canvas,
128 × 97 cm (50 ³/₈ × 38 ¹/₈ in).
Musée national du château, Versailles.

POMP AND INTRIGUE IN THE AGE OF LOUIS XIV

Hôtel de Lauzun

17 Quai d'Anjou

THE FIRST RECEPTION ROOM
This room contains the portrait
of Mademoiselle de Montpensier –
La Grande Mademoiselle –
by Mignard, as well as works
by Hubert Robert.

A SUITE OF ROOMS, OR 'ENFILADE'
Located on the second floor,
the suite comprises
two reception rooms,
the music room,
the bedchamber and the boudoir.

This famous Parisian mansion was built around 1657 on the occasion of the marriage of Charles Grouin (or Grüyn), son of an innkeeper on the Île de la Cité, the landlord of the 'Pomme de Pin' ('Pine Cone') in Rue de la Juiverie. Grouin had used his official post as Commissioner General of Supplies for the royal cavalry to amass great wealth and had been ennobled, assuming the title of Grouin des Bordes, Lord of Noizières, Lagny and other domains. His marriage contract specified that the mansion, then under construction, was to be the personal property of his new wife, Geneviève de Moüy.

Although Hôtel de Lauzun is one of the finest buildings in Paris and has survived virtually intact, the identity of the architect – even if the name of Louis Le Vau has been put forward – like that of the painters and sculptors involved, remains open to conjecture. The painted ceiling in the first-floor study features a *Triumph of Ceres* set amidst flat, gilded coffers with carved foliated scrolls. The staircase vault is embellished with *Time Discovering Truth*, painted in 1660 and stylistically somewhat reminiscent of Le Brun. Several of the second-floor rooms still retain their painted ceilings: in the Italianate music room can be seen a *Triumph of Venus*, while the alcove bedchamber has a *Diana and Endymion*, and in another small room the coved ceiling depicts a superb *Triumph of Flora*. Several portraits, genre scenes and still lifes were added in the 18th century. The interior decor features remarkable, gilded polychrome panelling in which can be discerned the influence of Simon Vouet, Pierre Patel and Eustache Le Sueur – who worked extensively at the neighbouring Hôtel Lambert.

Grouin was not destined to enjoy his fortune for long. Like many financiers who amassed sudden wealth, he was suspected of embezzlement and, during investigation of the Fouquet scandal, his own accounts were audited. He was found guilty and condemned to reimburse the king. Ruined and unable to pay a colossal fine, he was imprisoned and died in 1672. His widow had retained ownership of the mansion and passed it on to her son who, in 1682, sold it to Antonin Nompar de Caumont, Comte, and later Duc de Lauzun. Despite being an impoverished Gascon Cadet, Lauzun had managed to achieve prominence at court thanks to his relative, the Comte de Guiche. Small but handsome, he had become the lover of the Duchesse de Montpensier, the king's first cousin, known as 'La Grande Mademoiselle' (to distinguish

THE MUSIC ROOM
Carved wood panelling
and lavish gilding.

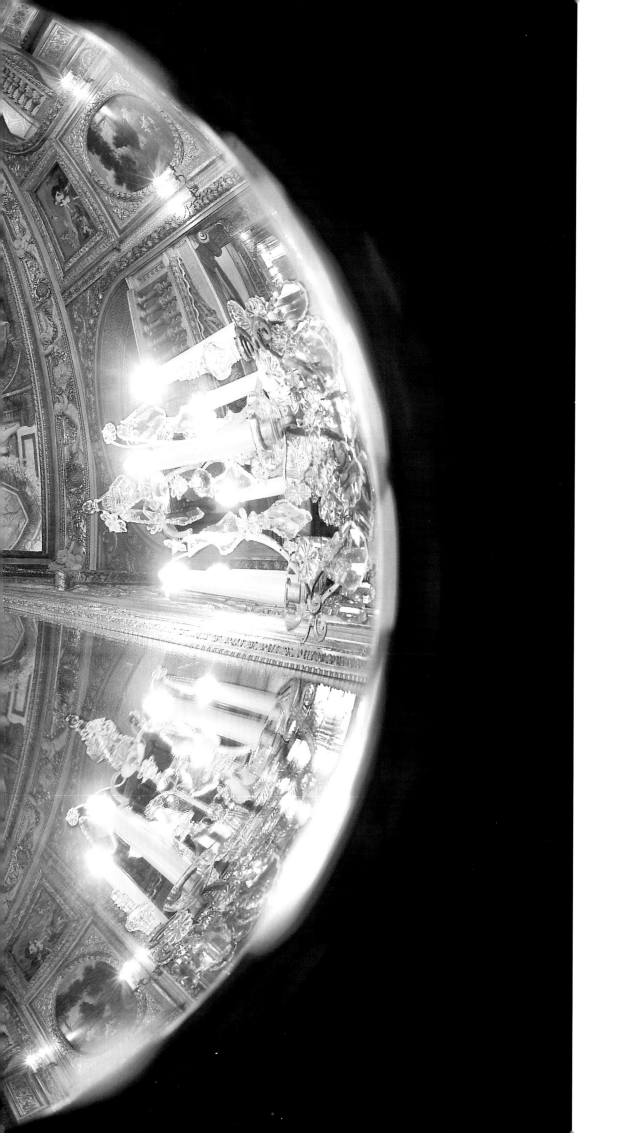

THE MUSIC ROOM

There are several painted
trompe-l'œil ceilings in Hôtel
de Lauzun; shown here,
The Triumph of Venus (c. 1658).

her from the other royal princesses rather than because of her stature). As she had been actively involved in the Fronde, Louis XIV had no great liking for her. Having sought to disregard the king's formal opposition to their marriage, which would have made him one of the most influential figures in the kingdom, Lauzun was temporarily exiled in the Piedmont fortress of Pignerol, or Pinerola, not far from Turin (at the time a French possession).

Set free in 1681, he bought the mansion which today bears his name from the heirs of Grouin des Bordes, and decided to live there with the Duchesse de Montpensier whom he ended up secretly marrying. But although the extraordinary couple were together at last, things did not go smoothly and they reputedly fought. It is not even certain that the Duchesse, of whom a fine portrait by Mignard hangs in one of the second-floor rooms, ever actually took up residence in the house.

Following his separation from La Grande Mademoiselle in 1684, Lauzun sold the property to the Marquis and Marquise de Richelieu. The mansion became a Mecca for Parisian libertines. The Marquis de Richelieu's father, Jean-Baptiste Amador Vignerod du Plessis, was seventeen when he abducted his future wife from her convent. A few years later, taking a leaf out of his father's book, Marquis Louis-Armand, the youngest of the Richelieu sons, in turn abducted Marie-Charlotte de la Porte du Theil, daughter of a Grand Master of Artillery and of Hortense Mancini, Cardinal Mazarin's niece, from the Convent of the Visitation in Chaillot where she had been sent as a boarder. In 1685, the newly-wed couple become owners of Hôtel de Lauzun where they held extravagant, ruinously expensive receptions and led amply fulfilled – but separate – love lives.

In his amorous proclivities, Louis-Armand de Richelieu was merely following in the family footsteps (and was indeed to be emulated in this respect by his own nephew, the future Maréchal de Richelieu). Unfortunately for the libertine, Mme de Maintenon and the *parti dévot* – partisans of strict religious observance – held sway at court; his debauched behaviour and mounting debts led to his exile. He joined the army, serving as colonel in a cavalry regiment, then ended his career as governor of the town of La Fère in the Aisne department. Separated *de facto* from her husband since 1695, and not unduly troubled by her predicament, the Marquise de Richelieu moved to London to lead her life as she saw fit, far from the influence of Mme de Maintenon and her clique. The grand-niece of Mazarin, she fully lived up to the tradition inaugurated at court by her own mother, Hortense, and by Olympe

Studio of Charles and Henri Beaubrun
MARIE-ANNE DE BOURBON-CONDÉ, DUCHESSE DE MONTPENSIER, KNOWN AS "LA GRANDE MADEMOISELLE".
n.d., oil on canvas, 130 × 98 cm
(51 1/8 × 38 5/8 in).
Musée Carnavalet, Paris.

THE BEDCHAMBER
Lower door panel.

and Marie-Anne Mancini, her aunts: "As fair as a Greek goddess", Saint-Simon tells us, "she became celebrated for the hectic pace at which she conducted her wandering existence."

In 1707, the mansion was acquired by Pierre-François Ogier d'Enonville, tax-collector for the Clergy, and remained in his family for sixty years. Its libertine reputation became a thing of the past, and the silken dresses of the Marquise de Richelieu's friends gave way to cassocks and surplices and then to the parliamentary robes worn by the friends of President Jean-François Ogier, son of Pierre-François. Germain Brice, invited to Hôtel de Lauzun in 1752, marvelled at the luxurious interior: "A house which, from the outside, is little different from its neighbours... but the apartments are magnificently lavish, overflowing with gilt..."

In 1769, it was acquired by the Maréchal de Tessé's son, and subsequently by the Marquis de Pimodan. The latter's daughter lived there during the Terror and is said to have hidden in an underground passage leading to the banks of the Seine while the police were searching the house. When Baron Jérôme Pichon, an official at the Council of State, installed his collections and library there, Hôtel de Lauzun became a focal rendezvous for artistic and literary circles. Having restored the residence, the new owner rented out part of the property to writers such as Charles Baudelaire and Théophile Gautier, and artists such as the painter Fernand Boissard. The latter inaugurated 'The Hashish Smokers' Club' in the large second-floor reception room where members would sample the delights of 'artificial paradise'.

The City of Paris purchased the property in 1900, then sold it back to Louis Pichon, the baron's grandson, who entirely restored the mansion before once again selling it to the City of Paris in 1928.

THE RIVAL

Hôtel de Soubise

60 Rue des Francs-Bourgeois

Charles and Henri Beaubrun |
**PORTRAIT OF ANNE DE ROHAN-CHABOT,
PRINCESSE DE SOUBISE**
N.d., oil on canvas, 78 × 61 cm (30 ⅝ × 24 in).
Musée national du château, Versailles.

In 1704, the Prince de Soubise commissioned the architect Pierre-Alexis Delamair to build him a mansion in the Marais district on the site of Olivier de Clisson's former manor house, built in 1380, and of the Renaissance mansion built for the Guise family. The architect was requested to conserve, wherever possible, the vestiges of the two earlier residences and these were fairly harmoniously incorporated into the new design. Taking the mansion of the Prior Superior at the Temple as his model, Delamair laid out a vast forecourt framed by a colonnade in the Composite order; this was surmounted by a balustraded promenade and culminated in a hemicycle on the site of the old Guise riding-school, in the present-day Rue des Francs-Bourgeois. The riding-school had formerly been separated from the Guise mansion by a small street called Rue de La Roche, still used as a public thoroughfare. One can well imagine the Prince de Soubise's exasperation as he stood at his windows watching the daily sight of cartloads of hay and bellowing livestock trundling across the courtyard below. The magnificent architectural ensemble formed by the roof-top sculptures – *Prudence, Wisdom,* and *The Spirits of the Arts* – and those standing between the upper-storey windows on the façades – *The Four Seasons,* copies of Robert Le Lorrain – can still be admired today.

No sooner had she arrived at Louis XIV's court than the Prince de Soubise's wife posed a genuine threat to Mme de Montespan, the king's acknowledged mistress. Red-haired, "with the fairest complexion in the world, a handsome face, but small eyes", the Princess, judging by the portrait of her belonging to the Versailles collections, was more than able to show herself off to advantage. In fits of jealousy, Mme de Montespan used to claim that she had "tainted blood and a body covered in ulcers".

HABOT·DE·ROHAN·PRINCESSE
DE SOVBISE

| Pages 74 and 75
THE OVAL RECEPTION ROOM
| The Princesse de Soubise's reception
room, decorated by Germain Boffrand
c. 1730, with paintings by Natoire
depicting the legend of Psyche
(1737).

Saint-Simon described her as "regularly attending court, impressing all those present, and having the upper hand over the ministers". In 1673, having successfully caught Louis XIV's eye, she was appointed lady-in-waiting. In the days when the king bowed to her every wish, she was often granted lengthy private audiences with him, "in the intimacy of the first study adjacent to the public reception room". Fully aware of his marital misfortune, the Prince de Soubise, so Saint-Simon informs us, "rarely appeared at court, absorbed himself in the management of his household affairs, and never betrayed the slightest suspicion, while his wife tactfully avoided any behaviour that was too conspicuous".

In 1712, following the death of the Soubises, the mansion was inherited by their son, Prince Hercule-Mériadec who, on the occasion of his second marriage in 1732, commissioned Boffrand to provide new interior decoration. Although the proportions of the entrance hall, stair-well and several of the rooms were conserved, tasteless alterations to the

decor were carried out under Louis-Philippe. On the other hand, the fine overdoors by Trémolières, Restout, Van Loo and Boucher have been retained in the Prince's main apartments, while the rococo reception room still has its panelling surmounted by eight stucco high-reliefs of allegorical figures attributed to Jean-Baptiste Lemoine and Lambert-Sigisbert Adam.

On the first floor, leading to the Princess de Soubise's apartments, is a vast antechamber where the *Concert des amateurs* used to take place. At these performances, the composer Gossec and the versatile Chevalier de Saint-Georges, who was of mixed race – a formidable fencer and, above all, accomplished violinist – would captivate elegant audiences with their music. The oval reception room, with its white and gold rococo panelling and its blue and gilt ceiling, is the finest room in the palace. A series of eight paintings by Natoire depicting the legend of Psyche hangs between the mirrors and windows.

| Pages 78 and 79
**VIEW, FROM THE PERISTYLE,
OF THE FAÇADE GIVING
ONTO THE MAIN COURTYARD**
| The mansion was built
between 1705 and 1708
by Pierre-Alexis Delamair.

The last owner was the libertine Charles de Rohan, known as the Maréchal de Soubise. He suffered from ill-health and in 1784 his nephew, Cardinal de Rohan, sought treatment from the notorious magician and physician Cagliostro. Both the Cardinal and Cagliostro, however, were implicated in the 'Diamond Necklace Affair', sparked off by their acquaintance the Comtesse de Lamotte. The Prince died in 1787 leaving a somewhat debt-burdened inheritance.

During the French Revolution, the building was used to store gunpowder seized from the Bastille, and then later served as a barracks for hussars. The heirs of the Rohan-Soubise family recovered the property under the First Empire and sold it to the state. In 1808 the National Archives were installed in the premises under their first curator, Daunou.

THE MAIN COURTYARD

Laid out in a horseshoe shape,
it is surrounded by a peristyle
with 56 paired columns
and a terraced roof.

THE HEIGHT OF ELEGANCE

Hôtel Carnavalet

23 Rue de Sévigné

THE SOUTH AND WEST FAÇADES
The main section
of the building, designed
c. 1545 by Pierre Lescot,
features ornamental
bas-reliefs attributed
to Jean Goujon and
depicting the four seasons.

THE WEST FAÇADE
This features ornamental allegorical bas-reliefs by Van Obstal representing the four elements. On the left, *Air* and *Fire*.

Hôtel Carnavalet is the most famous of all the aristocratic mansions in the Marais, and nowadays houses the museum of the same name. In the 17th century it was already renowned as the residence of the celebrated Marquise de Sévigné, one of the most sparkling ladies at Louis XIV's court.

In 1545, Jacques de Ligneris, President of the Chamber of Inquiries, decided to have a residence befitting his high-ranking office built in the Marais. The magistrate, who had been posted abroad as royal ambassador to the Council of Trent, left instructions with the architect Pierre Lescot and the sculptor Jean Goujon. The entrance to the mansion was in Rue de la Culture-Sainte-Catherine (present-day Rue de Sévigné) and a courtyard – still existing, and containing a magnificent Coysevox statue of Louis XIV which was added later – led to the house. The mansion originally consisted of the main building, two small pavilions, the lower section of the left wing and the main entrance. The courtyard façade, one of the rare vestiges of Renaissance

architecture in Paris, has retained the harmonious proportions created by the mouldings and above all by the sculpted decoration, the most striking features of which are the four large allegorical representations of the seasons. Summer and Autumn are personified by two classical divinities – respectively Ceres and Bacchus, both with their traditional attributes – while Spring is represented by a young man bearing floral crowns and garlands and Winter by an old woman wrapped up in her coat. These bas-reliefs, surmounted by the signs of the zodiac, are the work of Jean Goujon's atelier.

In 1571, Hôtel de Ligneris was sold to Françoise de La Baume de Montrevel, widow of François de Kernevenoy – the Gallicized version of the Breton name Kernevenoc'h – "a very beautiful and charming widow" according to the ever well-informed Brantôme, suggesting that she may have been a 'merry' widow. Although the new owner

made few alterations to the mansion, she did have the coat of arms of her deceased husband's family inscribed in the cartouche over the main doorway. This coat of arms featured a carnival (*carnaval* in French) mask, still plainly visible; ever since, the mansion has been known as the 'Carnavalet'.

About a century later, the subsequent owner, Claude Boislève, commissioned François Mansart to 'modernize' and 'embellish' the building in an ambitious programme of work. Mansart added a new storey to the street façade and built the two wings surmounted by sculpted motifs which surround the courtyard. On the left, complementing Goujon's *Seasons,* can be seen the *Four Elements.* These bas-reliefs are attributed to Van Obstal, as are the figures on the right (above the entrance to the present-day museum). The precise significance of the latter sculptures remains enigmatic. They are perhaps intended to portray four

THE MAIN COURTYARD

The bronze statue of Louis XIV by Coysevox formerly stood in the courtyard of the Hôtel de Ville.

mythological goddesses – Juno, Hebe, Diana and Flora – or may again represent the four cardinal points. Mansart played such a key role in redesigning the mansion that he has been accused of having destroyed the fine Renaissance composition of the original building.

The work barely completed, Claude Boislève was about to move into his mansion when he was implicated in the Fouquet scandal, arrested and incarcerated in the Bastille. He was dispossessed of the property by Louis XIV who then auctioned it off. In 1677, the new owner rented it to Marie de Rabutin-Chantal, widow of the Marquis Henri de Sévigné who had come to an untimely end as the result of a duel. Although Mme de Sévigné had already lived in several mansions in the Marais district, she had never found one which suited her. As soon as she heard that Hôtel Carnavalet was due to be leased, she set her heart upon it. Her impatience is revealed in her correspondence of September 1677; and on 7 October she triumphantly announced to her daughter that she had obtained the lease: "Thank God, we've got Hôtel de Carnavalet! It's a marvellous arrangement: there's room for all of us and we'll be the height of elegance. As we can't expect every-thing, we'll have to do without parquet floors and fashionable little chimney pieces. But we'll have a fine courtyard and a beautiful garden in a select district, and we'll be together, and you love me my dear child!" The mansion was indeed spacious and the layout ideal: "The house is so large", Mme de Sévigné also wrote to her daughter, "that even accommodating my son will be no problem. There are four coach houses and space for a fifth; stables are provided for eighteen horses... The garden is absolutely beautiful and well-tended." For the next twenty years, the sparkling marquise reigned over her fine man-sion, playing hostess to the congenial, brilliant social set chronicled in her delightful correspondence. She lived there until her death in 1696 which occurred in Grignan, at the home of her daughter whom she occasionally visited.

In the course of the 18th and 19th centuries, Hôtel Carnavalet belonged in turn to a succession of different families until July 1866, when the last owner sold the mansion to the City of Paris. On 23 June 1898, a museum devoted to the history of Paris was inaugurated on the premises by the President of the French Republic, Félix Faure.

THE CARTOUCHE ABOVE THE MAIN ENTRANCE
Detail of the Kernevenoy family coat of arms, surmounted by a sculpted *Abundance* perched on the carnival mask from which the popular name 'Carnavalet' derives.

THE ENCHANTING POISONER

Hôtel de Brinvilliers

12 Rue Charles-V

THE GRAND STAIRCASE
Detail of the listed wrought-iron
banister dating
from the 17th century.

THE ENTRANCE HALL
Thiais stone diamond paving.

Jean Restout the Younger, after Lebrun
THE MARQUISE DE BRINVILLIERS
1676, black chalk drawing
with white highlights,
34 × 24 cm (13 ³/₈ × 9 ³/₈ in).
Musée Carnavalet, Paris.

In the early years of Louis XIV's reign, in an elegant residence in the little Rue Charles-V, tucked away in the heart of the Marais district, lived the Marquise de Brinvilliers, an enchantingly beautiful young woman who was destined to become the most celebrated poisoner of her day.

Many a time the grimacing faun's mask surmounting the massive vault of the carriage entrance must have witnessed the notorious marquise's closed coach as it pulled out to a rendezvous with one of her lovers, or with the shadowy figure who supplied her with love philtres and deadly potions. Hôtel de Brinvilliers belonged to Antoine Gobelin, Marquis de Brinvilliers, who was living there at the time of his marriage in 1651. His wife stayed there intermittently after she decided to live separated from her husband whom she had wed in a marriage of convenience.

Marie marguerite d'Aubray marquise de Brinvillier eut la teste coupée,
son Corps brulé en place de Greve le 16 juillet 1676. cette fameuse Empoisoneuse a eté
dessinée par Mr. Restout sur le trait qu'en fit Mr. le Brun, lors qu'on la menoit au suplice.

She was small, delicate and extremely gracious. According to malicious rumour, since the tender age of seven she had indulged in other sins than greed. M. de Brinvilliers had unfortunately introduced into the privacy of the newly-weds' household an officer, Gaudin de Sainte-Croix, a handsome young gentleman from the south of France and a 'love child', as illegitimate offspring were called in those days. Mme de Brinvilliers soon warned her husband of their lodger's advances towards her, but the marquis placed his trust in the virtue of his young wife who, indeed, was regarded as a paragon of Christian piety and charity in the Marais district.

Nevertheless, M. de Dreux d'Aubray, less tolerant than his son-in-law, applied for a *lettre de cachet* and one fine morning Gaudin de Sainte-Croix was hustled off to the Bastille. There, the dashing young gallant made the acquaintance of an Italian who claimed to be an apothecary, skilled in the concocting of drugs of all kinds. As soon as he was freed from prison, Sainte-Croix sought to renew contact with his little marquise who was still enamoured and had not forgotten him.

In autumn 1666, M. de Dreux d'Aubray, infuriated by the scandal, retired along with his daughter to his country seat, the Château d'Offémont near Attigny in the Ardennes, in the hope that she might bid farewell to thoughts of her suitor. A few months later, the elderly gentleman succumbed – according to the local doctor – to "an acute attack of gout". Then some biscuits served up at a family meal whisked away the marquise's two brothers and her sister to be reunited with their father in a more perfect world. Who could have possibly suspected Mme de Brinvilliers? Outwardly, she continued to maintain an appearance of strict piety and, as a charitable lady with free access to the Hôtel-Dieu hospital, she could experiment with Gaudin de Sainte-Croix's drugs on the patients unimpeded. To cap it all, she was genuinely devout! However, Sainte-Croix himself died suddenly at his home in Place Maubert in July 1672 in the midst of the phials littering his secret laboratory. Whether or not his death was due to having tasted one of the marquise's little biscuits will never be known.

Sainte-Croix's house was about to be sealed by the investigating authorities when a somewhat breathless Mme de Brinvilliers turned up at the scene, insisting that she be allowed to reclaim a casket belonging to her. Confronted with the refusal of the police commissioners, she returned home, packed her clothes and jewellery and fled to Flanders that very evening. The casket contained correspondence sufficiently compromising to warrant her arrest. Although she discovered an

THE STAIRWELL
The stairwell and banisters with 'French-style' paving.

apparently safe hiding-place in a convent, a wily police officer, disguised as a priest, managed to sneak into the convent, lure her out and lead her back to Paris under guard. Mme de Brinvilliers made a full confession, admitting that she was responsible for the death of her relatives. After being subjected to mandatory torture, she continued to accuse herself, even exaggerating the extent of her responsibility. On 16 July 1676, at six o'clock in the evening, she was executed, Place de Grève – present-day Place de l'Hôtel-de-Ville – after having made amends, dressed in a chemise with a rope around her neck, at Notre-Dame cathedral. A huge crowd thronged to the execution place. According to Mme de Sévigné, her "poor little body was thrown into a large pyre after execution and her ashes scattered to the wind". The following day, curious passers-by came to rake through what remained of the victim's ashes looking for bones to carry off as relics of a woman who some were beginning to regard as 'blessed'. But the Marquise de Brinvilliers' execution did not, as it turned out, serve as a dissuasive example: a few months later, royal authority was profoundly shaken when the 'affair of the poisons' – with its combination of criminal activities and political intrigue – exploded like a bombshell. Mme de Montespan and several court ladies were implicated and exiled.

The mansion in Rue Charles-V was seized by the marquise's creditors and sold off. A few years later, it was there that Antoine Galland made the first translation from Arabic into French of the famous collection of tales, *The Arabian Nights' Entertainments*. Nowadays, the building is divided into apartments.

**THE FAÇADES OVERLOOKING
THE COURTYARD AND GARDEN**
The ensemble was built
in the 17th and 18th centuries.

THE INCONSTANT WIFE

Hôtel Aubert de Fontenay

5 Rue de Thorigny

THE COURTYARD FAÇADE
The mansion was built by Jean Boullier
de Bourges between 1656 and 1660.
The façade is crowned by a pediment
with carved dogs – an allusion
to Aubert's love of hunting.
The courtyard is framed by buttress
walls surmounted by female sphinxes.

In the 17th century Rue de Thorigny lay at the heart of the fashionable Marais district, an area to which elegant Parisian society had flocked since the latter years of Henri IV's reign. The Marais even boasted a public square named in honour of Louis XIII – present-day Place des Vosges which, until the Revolution, was known as Place Royale.

The inhabitants of the district included the cream of French aristocracy, wealthy magistrates, courtesans such as Ninon de Lenclos, and a large contingent of nouveaux riches. The latter were easily recognizable by the ostentatious extravagance of their dress, their carriages and, in the case of the wealthiest among them, their mansions. Salt-tax inspector Pierre Aubert was one such nouveau riche who sought to emulate the lifestyle of the grand aristocrats. Although in his seventies, he had effortlessly obtained the hand of a ravishing young lady, the daughter of Anne Chastelain, Lord of l'Essartine, and Madeleine Donon. To erase all trace of his common birth, he had purchased land at Fontenay-en-Brie and had his new estate elevated to the status of marquisate. Then, to please his young, attractive and ambitious wife, he commissioned the building of one of the three finest town houses in the Marais. Germain Brice mentions that this mansion, built between 1656 and 1660 by Jean Boullier – known as Jean Boullier de Bourges – was called Hôtel Salé (or 'Salted Mansion') in allusion to the official post held by the owner whose task was to levy the salt tax. The new building amply matched the social aspirations of the nouveau-riche couple; comfort and privacy took second place to the provision of vast, stately rooms. The apartments have painted panelling and four decorative overdoors by Coypel: *The Judgement of Paris*, *Diana at her Toilette*, *The Rape of Europa* and *The Abduction of Proserpine*. There are allusions to Aubert's love of dogs, both in the paintings and in the decorative motif beneath the cartouche on the pediment of the main courtyard façade which stands between the two large female sphinxes surmounting the lateral galleries. Leading to the upper floors is an impressive monumental staircase with a majestic frontispiece of Corinthian pilasters on top of which stand classical busts framed in medallions. The Baroque ornamentation and sculpture include two medallion busts, most probably representing the greybeard Aubert accompanied, on his right, by his young – but inconstant – wife.

Indeed, the name of Mme Aubert de Fontenay has come down in the annals of licentious living and the chronicler Tallemant des Réaux offers an uninhibited account of her notorious behaviour, at which the whole district poked fun. Her amorous reputation even spread beyond the frontiers of France and the Italian Marquis Giovanni-Battisti Pallavicini,

whom someone had roguishly informed that one merely had to be alone with Mme Aubert for her immediately to surrender her charms, wished to test the truth of such rumours. Hastening to Paris, the gullible marquis managed to get himself invited to the lady's home on some pretext or other. Tallemant des Réaux describes the ensuing scene as if he had witnessed it in person: "As soon as he found himself alone with Mme Aubert, he shrewdly bolted the door; in his broken French, he declared that he had long been in love with her and, now that an opportunity presented itself, had no intention of letting it slip away. At first she laughed, but when she saw that he was 'overheating', candidly informed him that if he did not withdraw she would douse him with so many pails of water that he would soon cool off…"

On a later occasion, Mme Aubert's charms were to 'overheat' a handsome Gascon, a swashbuckling relative of Mme de Montespan called César-Auguste Gondrin de Pardailhan, but who styled himself Marquis de Termes. She became totally infatuated with him and, once again, the contemporary chroniclers had a field-day: "The unfortunate Mme Aubert was besotted for so long that she married off her niece [Marie], daughter of her brother [Claude] Chastelain to the son of the dashing, but impecunious gentleman. It was a bad bargain. Ever since, Termes has such a hold over old Aubert that the poor fellow swears by him. Termes rules the roost. [...] With appalling ingratitude, he has ousted the lady [Madame Aubert] from any say in running the household. She has been left penniless."

When Aubert died, the mansion was still not completed. An interminable legal wrangle involving his widow, the Marquis de Termes, and the widow's niece Marie Chastelain, wife of the latter' son ensued. Finally, in 1674, it was Marie Chastelain who became the owner of Hôtel Salé. She rented it out to the Venetian ambassadors for three years and then, in 1705, sold it to her creditors.

In the mid-18th century, Thiroux de Chammeville bought Hôtel Salé as a gift for his daughter, wife of the Marquis de Juigné. The latter made the property over to his brother, Mgr de Juigné who, in 1781, became Archbishop of Paris, the last to occupy the see before the outbreak of the French Revolution. The monumental staircase was then hung with red velvet and the painted nudes were discreetly 'clothed'.

Hôtel Salé was sequestrated during the Revolution and rented out to the École centrale des arts et manufactures. Today, it houses the Picasso Museum.

A Foolhardy Cardinal

Hôtel de Rohan-Strasbourg

87 Rue Vieille-du-Temple

The fourth, last, and most celebrated Cardinal de Rohan, Louis-René-Édouard de Rohan-Guéméné, is notorious for his uninhibited private life and for the scandalous role he allegedly played in the so-called 'Diamond Necklace Affair' a few years before the Revolution. The Prince de Rohan-Guéméné, as he was known, had been Bishop of Strasbourg and subsequently a diplomat before finally being appointed Cardinal. His lavish lifestyle attracted a swarm of sycophants and various sleazy hangers-on. He initially created a scandal by publicly flaunting his affair with the Marquise de Ménars, Mme de Pompadour's sister-in-law, the first in a long succession of mistresses which was to culminate with Mlle Mayeul de Maningan, shortly before Rohan's flight as an émigré. It was through his good offices that Cagliostro had been summoned from Strasbourg to treat his ailing uncle, the Prince de Soubise, and then went on to establish a reputation in polite society. The 'magician' became a familiar visitor at Hôtel de Rohan, and even lodged there for a while before renting another nearby Marais town house in Rue Saint-Claude.

Although the Cardinal had been implicated in a number of shady speculative property deals, notably involving the Quinze-Vingts hospital, his eventual fall from grace was brought about by his foolhardy decision to throw in his lot in a scheme concocted by the enchanting Comtesse de Lamotte. Jeanne de Saint-Rémy was the direct descendant of an officially recognized bastard son of Henri II. Along with her sister, Jeanne had been sent to board in the Abbaye de Longchamp as an indigent gentlewoman. She escaped from the convent and, by around 1780, had moved to Bar-sur-Aube, where her family had formerly been great landowners. Comte Beugnot, a future high-ranking Napoleonic official, describes her as: "Slender and with a neat waist... she had extremely expressive blue eyes and black, sharply-curving eyebrows, a long face, a large, but admirably generous, mouth and, typical of such

features, a captivating smile. She had beautiful hands, dainty feet and a remarkably milky complexion." Gifted not only with physical charms, but with strength of character and resolute determination as well, Jeanne contrived to marry a certain M. de Lamotte who, although not wealthy, conveniently bore the title of count. She then sought to gain admittance to the queen's entourage at Versailles in order to have her claims to her ancestors' property recognized. Having experienced at first hand the court web of intrigue and petty corruption – based upon one's supposed influence with the princes and princesses – she was eventually recommended to Cardinal de Rohan. Within a few months, she and the Cardinal were on highly intimate terms and she more than once acted as hostess at his private receptions.

However, Jeanne wanted more than the magnificent gifts which the Cardinal showered upon her. Shrewdly noting that Rohan sought to win the queen's favour and coveted a ministerial post, the insatiable countess decided to use him as a pawn in an elaborate conspiracy. This involved Cardinal de Rohan financing the purchase of an extremely expensive diamond necklace which the countess was then supposed to deliver to Queen Marie-Antoinette on his behalf. The queen, however, was never to wear the necklace, for the very simple reason that Comtesse de Lamotte had meanwhile purloined it and had arranged for it to be broken up and sold off stone by stone! The conspiracy was exposed by the jewellers and the whole affair assumed distinctly political overtones when the queen vociferously claimed that she had been the innocent victim of a plot. All the protagonists were prosecuted and punished: the Lamottes were ultimately forced to flee to England, and Cardinal de Rohan was tried by a special court and exiled to La Chaise-Dieu from where he left for Germany, never again to set eyes upon the lady who had so cunningly tricked him. Jeanne, for her part, died in mysterious circumstances in London in 1791 while about to publish further revelations on what became known as the 'Diamond Necklace Affair'.

As befits a former prelates' residence (and excepting of course a certain prelate who was derisively dubbed 'Cardinal Carat'!) the present-day

THE 'CABINET DES SINGES'

Painted by Christophe Huet between 1749 and 1752.

Hôtel de Rohan has retained its unostentatious, somewhat stark appearance of old.

The original occupant was Armand-Gaston-Maximilien de Rohan, Prince-Bishop of Strasbourg, elected Cardinal in 1712. At the beginning of the 18th century, he had inherited from his parents some land bordering Rue Vieille-du-Temple. He decided to build a town house on the plot and commissioned the architect Delamair, along with sculptors who had worked on the decoration of the adjacent Soubise palace, separated only by large gardens. In appearance, however, Cardinal de Rohan's new mansion was more restrained than the stately residence belonging to his uncle and aunt, the Prince and Princesse de Soubise. The decorative sculptures, like the three first-floor windows on the main façade, are unassuming. The ensemble is crowned by a fine moulded pediment. Immediately to the right on entering the main

courtyard, a passageway leads to the famous stableyard known as the Courtyard of the Sun Horses, with its superb bas-relief by Robert Le Lorrain which depicts Apollo's rearing steeds coming to drink at sunset after their frenzied charge across the heavens.

The façade overlooking the garden extends across ten bays, the central section being highlighted by twin rows of four monumental columns on the ground floor and first storey. The interior has undergone considerable alterations since the initial design. The Company Room, or Music Room, has retained the original decor commissioned by the second Cardinal de Rohan, along with the overdoors painted by Jean-Baptiste Pierre, depicting scenes from the *Aeneid*. The suite of linking rooms on the first floor culminates in the 'Cabinet des Singes', dating from 1750, which contains a series of panels ostensibly depicting Chinese amusements, but treated rather in the style of Louis XV pastoral scenes attributed to Christophe Huet. In the upper sections of these panels, a light-hearted touch is provided by medallions featuring monkeys while the cornice is decorated with exotic birds.

Besides the Cardinal, responsible for building Hôtel de Rohan, and his descendant, the womanising, intrigue-prone Prince Louis, two other Rohans – both also Bishops of Strasbourg and Cardinals – meanwhile took up residence in the mansion. The first two were members of the French Academy. All four revelled in an extravagant, dashing lifestyle. During the Revolution, the mansion was sequestrated and looted before serving as a depot for the gunpowder previously stored at the Bastille. In 1808, the building was allocated to the Government Printing Office and the ensuing one hundred and twenty year-long 'industrial' occupancy wreaked considerable damage. The mansion was eventually restored in 1925 when the Printing Office vacated the premises.

| Voyé the Younger
PORTRAIT OF CARDINAL LOUIS-RENÉ DE ROHAN
| 1782-1789, etching,
| 25 × 18 cm (9 $^{7}/_{8}$ × 7 $^{1}/_{8}$ in).
| Musée des Arts décoratifs, Strasbourg.

2. The Faubourg Saint-Germain

THE COURTYARD FAÇADE
The mansion was rebuilt by Neveu
in the reign of Louis XVI.

FEMININE WILES, GRACE AND INTELLIGENCE

Hôtel d'Entragues

12 Rue de Tournon

THE COURTYARD FAÇADE
The mansion was rebuilt by Neveu
in the reign of Louis XVI.

THE STREET DOOR
Sculpted lion
on the main entrance.

Hôtel d'Entragues conjures up the memory of three women who, each in their own way, became prominent figures in their time. The first of these was Catherine-Henriette de Balzac d'Isliers, daughter of the Marquis François d'Entragues, Governor of Orleans, the owner – and no doubt builder in the early 17th century – of the two original mansions (the 'larger' and 'smaller' hôtels, located respectively at nᵒˢ 12 and 14 Rue de Tournon), and of Marie Touchet, Charles IX's great love. The beautiful lady, with whom Henri IV was infatuated, had been promised in marriage to the king under the terms of a contract – 'bill of sale' might perhaps be more appropriate – drawn up by her family on 1 October 1599. But despite her attractions and wiles, and the fact that she bore the king's child, she never actually became his lawfully wedded wife. "To tell the truth, Sire," she once snapped impatiently at her royal lover, "you stink like a rotting carcass!" To which the monarch retorted: "Indeed, my armpit does smell rather high!"

Tallemant des Réaux relates that when the king broke off the affair, "like Sardanapalus, she plunged into an excess of debauchery; obsessively stuffing herself with food, she grew monstrously obese. And yet

Jérôme Wierix |
**PORTRAIT OF CATHERINE-HENRIETTE
DE BALZAC D'ISLIERS D'ENTRAGUES,
MARQUISE DE VERNEUIL**
C. 1600, engraving.
Private collection, Paris.

| Jean-Baptiste Nini
**ALBERTINE-ELISABETH VAN NYVENHEIM VAN
NEUKIRCHEN, SUBSEQUENTLY MME PATER
THEN MARQUISE DE CHAMPCENETZ**
| 1768, terracotta medallion
with imitation boxwood patina,
diameter 16 cm (6 ¼ in).
| Private collection, Paris.

| E. V. (unidentified)
**ÉLISABETH DE LA LIVE DE BELLEGARDE,
COMTESSE D'HOUDETOT**
| Early 19th century, stipple engraving,
29 × 19 cm (11 ³/₈ × 7 ½ in).
| Bibliothèque nationale de France,
| cabinet des estampes, Paris.

she had a keen wit…" By way of compensation, Henri IV had conferred upon her the title of Marquise de Verneuil, but her bitterness was such that she was later even suspected of having had a hand in his assassination by Ravaillac. The d'Entragues family mansion passed down from father to son before finally being sold, in 1699, to a gentleman by the name of Rousseau who, in 1716, rented it to the Swedish Ambassador, Erik Sparre.

During the winter of 1762, fashionable Parisian and Versailles circles became intrigued by a mysterious lady who had arrived from the United Provinces on honeymoon with her husband. As the couple planned to remain in Paris for several months they had rented the huge Hôtel d'Entragues. From then on, there was a constant coming and going of emblazoned carriages in Rue de Tournon; an endless procession of insatiably curious gentlemen would alight at the door of the mansion in the hope of being introduced to the femme fatale. After a while, the door would be opened by her husband, a wealthy Dutch merchant by name of Pater, who would greet the callers, informing them: "Sirs, I appreciate the honour you pay me by your visit, but I am afraid you may well be disappointed as I spend the whole day with Madame and at night she shares my bed."

The focus of all this fascinated interest, Mme Pater, née Albertine-Elisabeth Van Nyvenheim Van Neukirchen, was probably Greuze's most beautiful model; her features have also been captured in works by other artists, such as the sculptor Nini. The sheer number of admiring suitors finally got the better of the couple's marriage: the husband returned to The Hague and his young wife went back to her parents in Gelderland to await the completion of legal separation formalities. Mme Pater subsequently reappeared in Paris. She had meanwhile become a millionairess plantation-owner in Surinam and was now known as Baronne de Neukirchen (or Nieukerque). Launching out to conquer high society, she almost managed to supplant Mme Du Barry in the affections – and bed – of Louis XV. But as a divorced, Protestant foreigner she could never aspire to become the royal favourite. As a reward for her accommodating attitude, however, the king granted

her life tenancy of an apartment in the royal château at Meudon; her place at court become official after her marriage to the old Marquis de Champcenetz, Governor of Meudon.

Following the departure of the blonde goddess, another woman took up residence in Hôtel d'Entragues. Unlike her predecessors, Mme d'Houdetot, who bought the mansion in 1765, was neither scheming nor beautiful, but on the other hand she was remarkably intelligent. When she died in 1813, ownership passed to her heirs-at-law who were still in possession at the end of the last century.

The Comtesse d'Houdetot, wealthy daughter of a farmer-general (royal tax-collector), commissioned the architect Neveu to carry out renovation work at Hôtel d'Entragues. In the large ground-floor room she then opened what became one of the most avant-garde salons in Paris, attended principally by the Encyclopaedists and philosophers. Diderot, who along with a few other guests once for all formed the nucleus of the gathering, described the start of one of the meetings at his friend's house in the following passage: "At noon, M. de Villeneuve arrived. We were in the magnificent reception room, the windows of which look out onto the garden. M. Grimm was having his portrait painted and Mme d'Épinay was leaning on the back of the chair of the person painting. In a corner of the room, M. de Saint-Lambert was reading the most recent pamphlet I had sent him. I was playing chess with Mme d'Houdetot. Dear old Mme d'Esclavelles was surrounded by all her children and was chatting with them and the governor."

In 1757, while Mme d'Houdetot's lover, Saint-Lambert, was away in Spain, Jean-Jacques Rousseau fell passionately in love with her, an incident which he refers to in his *Confessions*. She took a keen interest in the progress of the American War of Independence, and was made an honorary citizen of New Haven at the request of her old friend Benjamin Franklin.

One of her contemporaries summed up the secret of her charisma thus: "It will come as a consolation to unattractive-looking women to learn that Mme d'Houdetot, who was extremely ugly, owed the fact that she was so well and constantly beloved to her intelligence and, above all, to her charming personality."

THE FAÇADE OVERLOOKING THE GARDEN
After the alterations and embellishments
introduced by Comtesse d'Houdetot,
Hôtel d'Entragues became an important
society rendezvous under the Ancien Régime.

THE MISFORTUNES OF A LIBERTINE LADY

Hôtel de Rothelin-Charolais

101 Rue de Grenelle

Pierre Gobert |
PORTRAIT OF LOUISE-ANNE DE BOURBON-CONDÉ,
MADEMOISELLE DE CHAROLAIS
N.d., oil on canvas, 116 × 110 cm
(45 ⅝ × 43 ⅜ in).
Musée des Beaux-Arts, Orléans.

Philippe d'Orléans, Marquis de Rothelin, commissioned the building of this extremely classical mansion between 1700 and 1704, under the supervision of the architect Lassurance. The façade overlooking the courtyard presents an Ionic arrangement with a slightly-raised attic storey with pilasters. The pediment, which formerly bore the coat of arms of the original owner, is somewhat distorted by the rounded arch of the central window on the attic storey. The garden façade consists of a main two-storey section embellished with six Corinthian columns and flanked by lower wings. The arch of the central first-floor window encroaches on the pediment depicting a beautiful *Ceres* with two cherubim in attendance. Rothelin extended the property by acquiring several parcels of land, then fell into debt and was forced to sell it off to a Swiss banker, Hogguer, Baron de Presles. The banker, who was also a diplomat, enjoyed the king's full confidence, and this enabled him to keep his own creditors at bay. Among his expenses were the generous gifts he lavished on his mistress, the buxom Mlle Desmarres, who lived in a neighbouring town house in Rue de Varenne.

The mansion retained its classical arrangement until the arrival of Louise-Anne de Bourbon-Condé, Mademoiselle de Charolais, the elder sister and neighbour of Mlle de Sens. A forceful personality, she had obtained the right to bear the royal title of 'Mademoiselle', and led her life as she saw fit. She embarked upon a programme of work intended to give the building a majestic appearance befitting her own lofty rank. Wings were added at right angles to the courtyard façade, outbuildings were provided on annexed plots, and the entrance porch assumed its definitive form. Inside, a large reception room was laid out with rococo panelling featuring decorative flowery boughs; the *Seasons*

THE GARDEN FAÇADE
The mansion was built
by Lassurance
between 1700 and 1704.

Page 124 |
THE MAIN RECEPTION ROOM
The rococo panelling
with decorative flowery boughs
and the set of mirrors
in this room date from the days
of Mademoiselle de Charolais.

Page 125 |
THE YELLOW ROOM
This room was refurbished
in First Empire style when
the mansion was taken over
by the Ministry of the Interior.

were painted over the doors, occasional pier panels with ornamental stucco carving were provided, and there was no shortage of gilding. The mansion became a hive of social – and libertine – activity. Inspector Marais, whose task involved keeping a close eye on a number of high-ranking personalities, gave a fully-detailed account of the princess's private life, describing her as "vivacious and dashing", "extremely charming and utterly disparaged". One witness wrote in his Journal in May 1735: "On recent meat-eating days, she had many guests to supper, including the Comte de Coigny, son of the Maréchal, reputed to be having affair with her. After supper, she dismissed everybody. The little Duc de Nivernois, a young man of about fifteen or sixteen, was reluctant to leave. Obliged to comply however, he hid behind a door-curtain and was able to witness the 'tête-à-tête' between Mademoiselle and the Comte de Coigny. Rebuked by the princess, he took his revenge by composing a rather scurrilous song about her secret charms." The offensive ditty was published along with other assorted gossip, notably concerning the affair between Mademoiselle and the Abbé de Vauréal, Bishop of Rennes, whom she wished to have appointed Secretary of State for Foreign Affairs. The Marquis d'Argenson, who actually was Foreign Secretary, jokingly referred to the matter: "In the absence of her mitred lover, Mademoiselle is consoling herself as best she can with little Coigny. But the Bishop of Rennes is said to be a great payer of arrears. He has the makings of a cardinal. This is precisely what appeals to the princess who, already past her best and having provided so many services herself, has embarked early on the career of madam, deriving her esteem from this profession alone."

Following Mademoiselle de Charolais' death, the mansion remained relatively unchanged. The property was seized when her grand-nephew and heir, the Comte de La Marche, emigrated, and was then handed back to the Conti family at the Restoration. In 1825, Hôtel de Charolais was acquired by the Ministry of the Interior. Casimir Perier died on the premises from cholera in 1832, and when the Austrian Embassy occupied the premises between 1861 and 1869, Princess Pauline de Metternich held her salon there. It has been French state property since 1870.

THE MAIN RECEPTION ROOM

General view showing
the overdoors with paintings
of the Seasons.

The Distractions of a Young Princess

Hôtel de Noirmoutier

136 Rue de Grenelle

THE COURTYARD FAÇADE
Built by Jean Courtonne
in 1720.

Both the design and history of this charming, elegant mansion are typical of the residences in Faubourg Saint-Germain. In 1719 Antoine-François de la Trémoille, Duc de Noirmoutier, acquired a plot of land in Rue de Grenelle and commissioned the architect Jean Courtonne (who also designed Hôtel Matignon) to build him a new residence. In his *Treatise on Practical Perspective*, Courtonne writes: "The project of this illustrious noble, whose lofty birth was matched by his supremely consummate appreciation of the finest arts, had begun to take shape in 1720", omitting to mention that the Duc de Noirmoutier had been blind since the age of twenty, a fact which made his refined aesthetic taste all the more remarkable! According to the architect's specifications, the mansion was to consist of "a twin-section main building standing between the courtyard and garden with a façade measuring fifteen *toises* (90 feet) in length, and with two projecting pavilions on the courtyard side, one containing the main staircase, the other a private staircase; the section of the main building looking onto the courtyard is to have a large central room with a dining room on one side and a large bedchamber on the other; the other section looking onto the garden is to contain a large reception room with bedchambers on either side, and a chapel and wardrobe-room to the rear". The main building, set three feet above the paved courtyard, was to be surmounted by "a square-shaped attic storey with a layout identical to that of the main floor beneath". Moreover, on the garden side, two wings were to extend from the main building, while provision was to be made for "a carriage entrance with columns, and outbuildings housing the kitchen, stables and coach houses with servants' quarters above". The mansion was completed in 1724 without any notable modification to the initial project. "This latest house", according to one observer, "represents a notable embellishment to a district which, once unpopulated, is daily being filled with new buildings."

In 1733, following the death of the Duc and Duchesse de Noirmoutier, the property was acquired by Mlle de Sens (daughter of Louis II de Bourbon and Mlle de Nantes, herself the legitimized daughter of Louis XIV and Mme de Montespan) who, like her sister and other royal princes and princesses, had become captivated by the district. Élisabeth-Alexandrine de Bourbon-Condé, formerly Mlle de Gex and then, from 1707, Mlle de Sens, had such a passionate interest in science that she had a laboratory installed in her elegant mansion; her richly-stocked library bore testimony to her cultivated taste, notably

THE COURTYARD FAÇADE
Detail of the balcony supported by impressive consoles decorated with lions' heads. The ground-floor windows are surmounted by ornamental mascarons (grotesque faces).

Pages 130 and 131 |
THE FAÇADE OVERLOOKING THE GARDEN

THE FIRST RECEPTION ROOM
Laid out in the axis
of the courtyard, this room
is linked directly to the state
apartment overlooking
the garden.

in horticulture and music. Along with her faithful lover, the Comte de Langeron, she led an energetic social life and the couple held lavish receptions at Hôtel de Noirmoutier. After the acquisition of adjacent plots of land, extension work was carried out and two new bays were added to the façade overlooking the garden. On 15 April 1765, Mlle de Sens died in the mansion which she had had sumptuously decorated by Lassurance. The sole vestige of this decor is the magnificent panelling depicting scenes from La Fontaine's *Fables*.

The building remained in the hands of the Condé family who rented it out until the Revolution, when it was seized and sold off as state property. From 1797, it was occupied for a while by Louvet de Couvray, former member of the Convention and author of the bawdy novel, *Les aventures du chevalier de Faublas*, who set up his bookshop there after having run a similar establishment in the Palais-Royal arcades. In 1814, the last owners sold it to the state. The elegant, still intact building was used initially to accommodate the bodyguards of 'Monsieur', the future Charles X, before being turned into the Army staff college and finally staff headquarters. In 1853, the wings on either side of the main building were raised. After the First World War, the mansion was placed at the disposal of Marshal Foch, who died there in 1929. Since 1970 it has been occupied by the Prefect of the Île-de-France Region.

DETAIL OF THE PANELLING
depicting one of
Jean de La Fontaine's fables.

THE FAIR LADY FROM INDIA

Hôtel de Gallifet

50 Rue de Varenne

THE GARDEN FAÇADE
This façade was built from 1775
to designs by the architect Legrand.
The monumental balcony
is supported by six half-engaged
Ionic columns.

In 1709, President Talon had a town house built on the former site of the Sainte-Croix cemetery between Rue de Grenelle and Rue de Varenne, with a main entrance in Rue du Bac. In 1766, the president's widow sold part of the gardens to the Marquis Louis-François de Gallifet, Baron de Preuilly. In 1775 this naval captain, whose dancing talents were much appreciated by Marie-Antoinette, commissioned the architect Legrand to build the splendid mansion which still stands today. The decoration was executed by Jean-Baptiste Boiston, the Prince de Condé's sculptor, who had already decorated the Château de Chantilly and the Palais Bourbon.

In his Parisian travel memoirs, Thierry gives a detailed description of the residence: "The main building stands at the back of the second courtyard, embellished by a large open peristyle composed of eight thirty-foot-high Ionic columns [...]. Set back to the left, another peristyle decorated with twenty Doric columns forms a covered passageway leading to the main staircase in the centre right. Oval in shape, its first storey is embellished with twelve Ionic columns, and it culminates in a dome decorated with arabesques and with a central opening to admit light." At the base of the dome a series of bas-reliefs, inspired by Ovid's *Metamorphoses*, can still be admired today. Externally, the uncompleted mansion offers a perfect example of late Louis XVI Italianate architecture: the façade overlooking the courtyard and its portico, like the garden façade, both consisting of columns of the Colossal order, represented a new style which began to be generally adopted in the last quarter of the 18th century.

In 1798, the prevailingly Neo-Classical interior decoration of Hôtel Gallifet was almost completely altered by the architects Augustin Renard and Montamant. The grand reception room was rearranged into two rooms embellished with mirrors. One room was provided with Ionic columns, the other with Corinthian, and they communicated by intercolumniation. Ornamental sculptures were reduced to a minimum and both ceiling covings and column fluting were simply painted in *trompe-l'œil*. The small reception room, also Ionic, featured charming bas-relief arabesques framing the central pier-glass.

Following the owners' departure, the mansion was sequestrated and then auctioned off under the laws governing émigré property. The government took possession of the building in 1790, but it was not until Ventôse in the Year II (March 1794) that it was assigned to the Ministry of Foreign Affairs. It was from there that the titular Minister, Charles Delacroix, father of the painter, conducted French foreign

**THE SEMI-CIRCULAR VESTIBULE
AND GRAND RECEPTION ROOM**
With their paired columns
and mirror effects, the salon
and vestibule together form
a vast reception room.

affairs between 1795 and 1797. Delacroix was succeeded by Talleyrand, who remained in office throughout the long period from July 1797 to 1807, save for a brief moment on the eve of the coup d'état of Brumaire in the Year VIII. Talleyrand's occupancy marked a revived period of splendour for Hôtel Gallifet. Lavish receptions were held, notably the revelries organized on 3 January 1798 to celebrate Bonaparte's victorious Italian campaign.

Talleyrand had no sooner taken up residence than he became attracted to a beautiful émigrée, Mme Grand, née Catherine Worlée. This diaphanous creature, English by education and culture, born in the Dutch Indies and wife of an international banker, had arrived in Paris in the mid-1780s with her English lover, the former Governor of Madras. Before emigrating in 1792, she had had numerous passing lovers, including Valdec de Lessart, Minister of Foreign Affairs under the Constituent Assembly. While in exile, she had hobnobbed with leading political circles in Britain and had had an affair with the Comte de Lambertye. She had returned to Paris in 1797 in an attempt to sort out her situation. Threatened with arrest, she sought the

**THE GRAND RECEPTION ROOM
AND VESTIBULE**

In the foreground, a basin supported
by tritons. The ceiling coving features
trompe-l'œil decorations.

François Gérard
**PORTRAIT OF CHARLES-MAURICE
DE TALLEYRAND-PÉRIGORD**
Early 19th century, oil on canvas.
Château de Valençay, Valençay.

protection of Talleyrand who was only too eager to help. He let her
stay for a while at his country seat in Montmorency, then installed her
in the private apartments of Hôtel Gallifet as his resident mistress.
Moreover, Talleyrand thought he might be able to use Mme Grand to
establish unofficial contacts with representatives of the British government – peace not yet having been signed with Great Britain. On his
behalf, she carried out a number of confidential missions to James
Crawford, the British chargé d'affaires in Hamburg. It later came to
light, however, that she was peddling her influence with Talleyrand
to foreign agents, lucrative operations from which her lover shame-
lessly profited. During the Consulate, under Mme Grand's 'reign',
Hôtel Gallifet became a hub of cosmopolitan social life; the cream of
European diplomatic or business circles flocked there, along with the
most attractive and sparkling women in Paris such as Mmes Visconti,
de Bonneuil, Gay or de Montrond. Enjoined by Bonaparte to choose
between his ministerial office and his mistress, the former Bishop of
Autun made all the necessary arrangements to marry his 'fair Indian
lady'. Shortly afterwards, the First Consul remarked in conversation to
the latter: "I do hope Mme de Talleyrand will manage to consign
Mme Grand to oblivion!" "I could do no better in that respect", she
replied, "than to take citizeness Bonaparte as my example."

Under the Restoration, the mansion was returned to the Gallifet
heirs who rented it out to the state. The Ministry of Foreign Affairs
remained there until moving to Quai d'Orsay in 1821. Nowadays,
Hôtel de Gallifet houses the Italian Embassy.

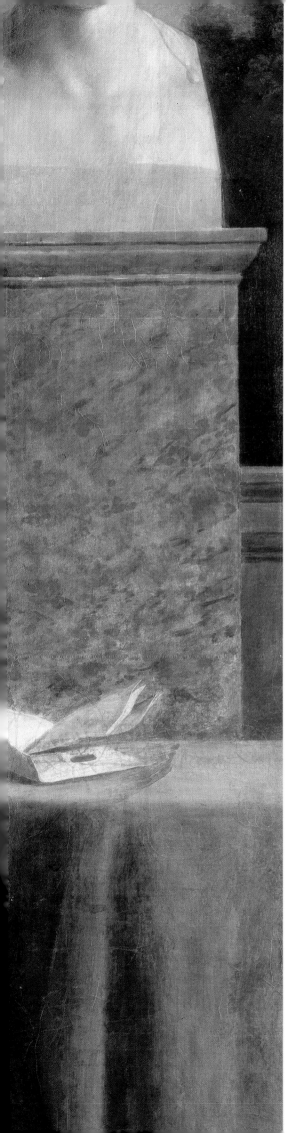

THE PALACE OF 'MADAME MÈRE'

Hôtel de Brienne

14 Rue Saint-Dominique

| François Gérard
**PORTRAIT OF MARIE LETIZIA
RAMOLINO BONAPARTE**
1803, oil on canvas,
215 × 145 cm (84 ⅝ × 57 ⅛ in).
Musée national du château, Versailles.

This residence and its outbuildings were built by President Duret, better known as an entrepreneur than as a parliamentary magistrate. Duret entrusted the plans and supervision of the work, commissioned in 1723 by the Marquise de Prie, the Duc de Bourbon's favourite, to the architect Aubry. Without giving any prior warning, the marquise suddenly pulled out of the project even though the owner of the plot of land on which building work had already begun, the Comte de Beaujeu, had not yet been paid. Moreover, on an adjacent plot, Duret had meanwhile launched work on a second, smaller mansion. Luckily, he simultaneously found two buyers, the Duchesse de La Vrillère for the larger house, and the Comte de Clermont d'Amboise for the other. Work resumed and new interiors in the 'Chinese' style were commissioned. The sculptor Michel Lelièvre worked on the apartment of the Comtesse de Saint-Florentin, the Duchesse de La Vrillère's daughter-in-law, while his colleagues Herpin and Pelletier designed remarkable cabinets with lacquered panels and mirrors.

In 1735, both mansions were acquired by Louise-Élisabeth de Bourbon, dowager Princesse de Conti and widow of Louis-Armand, at a period when royal princes and princesses were succumbing to the charms of the Faubourg Saint-Germain.

The large mansion, in which four of the reception rooms are listed, has retained its original high portal, its Tuscan ground floor designed by Aubry, and its Ionic first storey surmounted by a large triangular pediment standing on twin orders of pilasters. At the rear, the casement windows overlook a majestic garden which sweeps down to Rue de l'Université; it was one of the largest gardens in the street and was provided with flower-beds facing the main building, small lodges, groves, a summer house and even a maze. When, after having lived there for forty years, the dowager Duchesse de Conti died on the premises, the two mansions formed part of the same property. Both buildings were inherited by her nephew, the Comte de La Marche, who took possession of them in 1775 and then proceeded to sell them off separately. The large mansion was acquired and lived in by the Comte de Brienne and his famous brother, Étienne-Charles Loménie de Brienne, Archbishop of Toulouse and later Louis XVI's Minister of Finance, who proved incapable of setting French affairs in order again following the departure of Calonne. From 1776 onwards, several members of the family lived in the house, including the extremely attractive Vicomtesse de Canisy, née Marie-Anne de Loménie, a friend of the Condorcets, who was a regular hostess at the receptions held by her uncle, the Archbishop and Minister. Although the Loménie de Brienne family had new alterations carried out, they left in place the decors which dated from the days of the Marquise de La Vrillère, along with the numerous paintings by Oudry which the Princesse de Conti had commissioned.

Hôtel de Brienne was sequestrated and then handed back to the Comtesse de Brienne, the sole survivor of the family which had been executed during the Terror – all beheaded along with the king's sister, Madame Élisabeth, on 10 May 1794. That same year it was taken over by the state and sold. In July 1802, it was bought by Lucien Bonaparte. Following his secret marriage to Mme Jouberthon, however, he was packed off to Italy by his elder brother Napoleon, outraged by such gross insubordination. A little door had even been built into the garden wall of the mansion running along Rue de l'Université for the convenience of Mademoiselle Georges when she called on Lucien Bonaparte!

In 1806, Napoleon installed his mother in the mansion and it was somewhat pompously designated the 'Palace of Madame Mère'. Letizia

THE YELLOW ROOM
The drawing-room of Letizia Ramolino,
Napoleon Bonaparte's mother.

Ramolino, of Corsican origin, had been extremely attractive and flirtatious in her youth. Without parental approval, she had married Charles Bonaparte, a distinguished lawyer of venerable Genoese stock, and had borne him thirteen children including five sons. Widowed in 1785, Mme Bonaparte encountered immense hardship in providing for the needs of her offspring but was taken under the wing of the Comte de Marbeuf, the last governor of Corsica, who arranged for her sons to be educated in Paris. During the Revolution, once more plagued by inextricable difficulties, she had taken refuge in Marseilles when British forces seized Corsica. She was to remain forever haunted by the memory of those years of hardship and humiliation. This may well account for her reputed parsimony and thrift even at a time when, thanks to her son Napoleon, she had attained the pinnacle of wealth and honours. When the Empire was declared, she received the title of 'Madame Mère', and was provided with her own mansion and a private income sufficient to maintain her lofty status. Napoleon appointed her Protectress-General of charitable institutions, an official charge which she fulfilled with the discernment born of experience. Madame Mère was probably the only person who dared stand up to Napoleon and to reproach him openly in a manner which he would not even have tolerated from the Empress. Following the collapse of the Imperial regime, she left for Rome where she lived in seclusion until her death in 1836.

The well-conserved Hôtel de Brienne includes a magnificent reception room, known as the 'Blue Room', with white and gold panelling. The 'Red Room' has a *trompe-l'œil* decor and its various panels feature yellow and bistre ornamental arabesques enhanced with gilding. On the first floor, a few vestiges of the original decor remain, notably a boudoir which was once part of Madame Mère's apartments, with gilded reliefs set against a straw-coloured background.

At the Restoration, the mansion was taken over by the Ministry of War and in February 1817 the first official occupant, General Clarke, Duc de Feltre, took up residence.

THE COURTYARD FAÇADE
Designed by Aubry (1724),
President Duret's architect.

AN IMPERIAL RESIDENCE

Hôtel de Beauharnais

78 Rue de Lille

THE 'SEASONS ROOM'
The paintings of the Seasons
are attributed to Boisfremont.

THE MUSIC ROOM
The Empire style decorative
panels representing
the Muses are attributed
to Girodet.

A masterpiece of the First Empire style, Hôtel de Beauharnais – which owes its name to Empress Joséphine's son – has survived intact. Both the interior decor and the custom-designed furniture for its reception rooms and bedchambers have been miraculously conserved (a particularly rare occurrence in the case of furniture), due to the fact that, since 1818, the building has successively housed the Prussian Legation and the German Embassy.

It was built in 1713 by the architect Germain Boffrand, the original owner. It then passed through various hands – two notable owners being Colbert's nephew and Mme de Tencin, renowned for her salon – before being acquired by the Duc de Villeroy in 1780. The latter aristocrat was guillotined in 1794 and the mansion sold off as state property.

On 20 May 1803, Prince Eugène de Beauharnais bought the former Hôtel Boffrand from its most recent owners. Converted meanwhile into a 'low-rent middle-class residence', it had become rather dilapidated and had lost much of its former splendour. To accommodate such a grand personage as Napoleon Bonaparte's stepson its lustre had to be restored. Advised by his mother Joséphine, who combined aesthetic discernment with a taste for the luxurious, Eugène had the mansion totally redesigned, retaining only the four walls and grand staircase of the original building. Percier and Fontaine provided the magnificent decors. In a letter to his stepson in 1806, the Emperor, who kept a watchful eye on everything, did not fail to upbraid him for his negligence and

The music room
Detail
of a decorative panel.

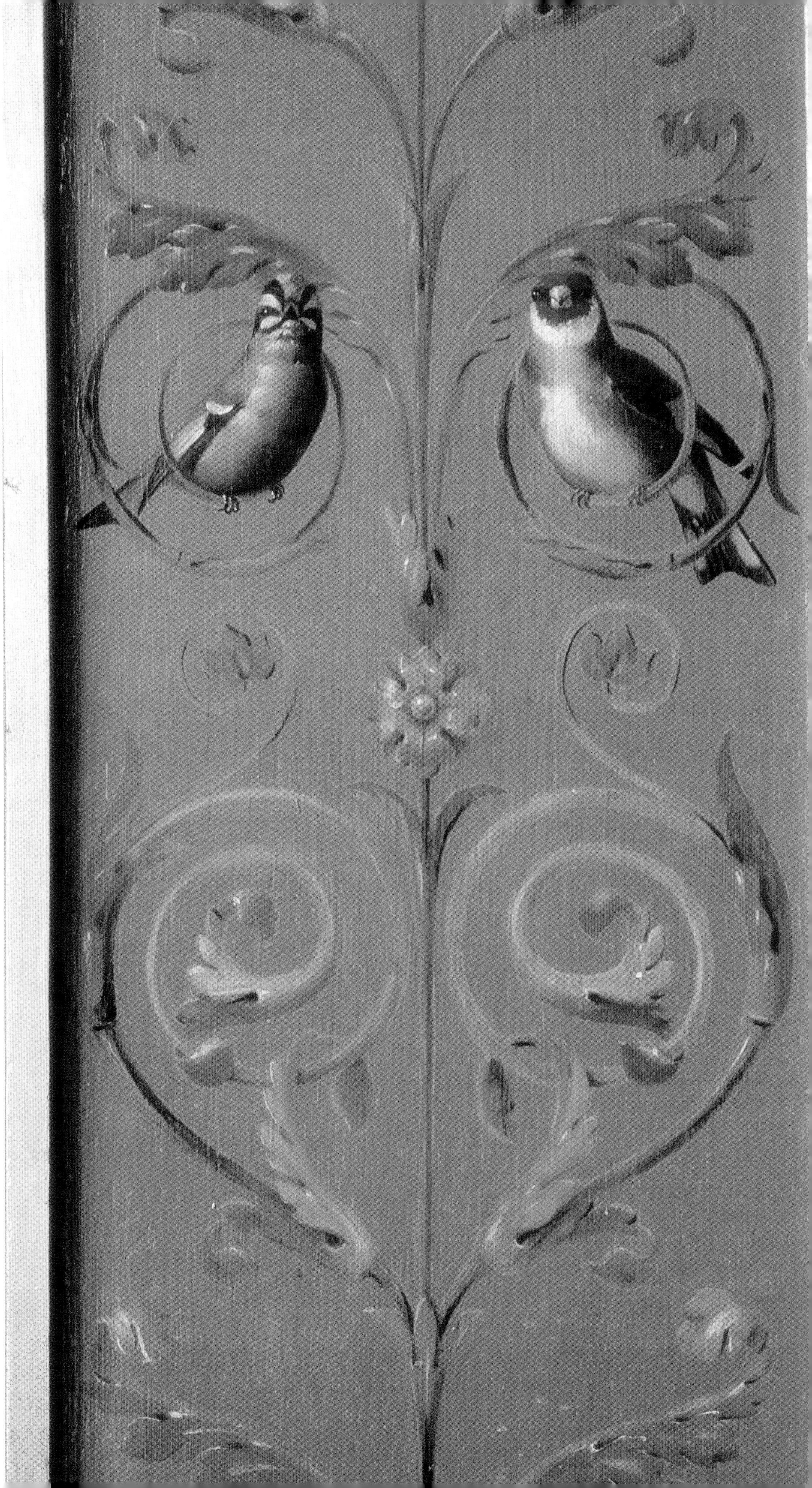

Right-hand page
The bedchamber
Panel featuring
a sylph.

for the enormous expense involved in the new decoration and layout of the mansion. "You've already spent more than one and a half million and have received little in return, you're dealing with a bunch of rogues, let me take care of the matter" is in substance what this letter said. And indeed, the formidable stepfather went on to take charge of everything, curbing expenses, firing the clerk of works and trimming down the estimates. Nevertheless, the amount of money spent on the furnishings was still very impressive for the times.

As Viceroy of Italy, Eugène de Beauharnais was to spend little time in the sumptuous residence which had been so painstakingly redecorated. Napoleon granted him no respite and the prince was only in Paris on rare occasions. Even then, he did not stay in his own mansion. His step-father, a regular tyrant where domestic affairs were concerned, regarded Hôtel de Beauharnais as his personal property and freely availed himself of the premises to accommodate various visiting dignitaries as changing policy requirements dictated. In 1810, Eugène's sister, Queen Hortense of Holland, separated from her husband Louis Bonaparte, was allowed to move into the mansion and her memory still lingers on in some of her favourite rooms. She received her close friends, surrounded herself with a dazzling entourage and held lavish parties. The bedchamber, known as the 'Queen Hortense bedchamber', is the

THE BEDCHAMBER
Known as the 'Queen Hortense bedchamber', it is a masterpiece of Empire style interior decoration.

THE MUSIC ROOM
Frieze with a motif of garlands and swans.

| François Gérard
PORTRAIT OF QUEEN HORTENSE
1810-1815, oil on canvas,
65 × 55 cm (25 ⅝ × 21 ⅝ in).
Musée national du château de la Malmaison
| et de Bois-Préau, Rueil-Malmaison.

crowning feature in the residence. It is decorated in a very pure, unassuming, yet exquisite style, with silk hangings studded with golden stars on a bluish-grey background. The Queen of Holland's state bed – a masterpiece of the Empire style – is surrounded by exotic wood veneered doors, the panels of which bear painted attributes in medallions. There are also two admirable little adjacent rooms: a Turkish boudoir and a bathroom which, although very small, has been designed with an artful interplay of mirrors creating an illusion of infinite space. In 1814, Frederick William III, King of Prussia, lived in Hôtel de Beauharnais during his stay in Paris. On his departure, the Prussian Legation remained in the premises. In 1817, Count Golz was entrusted with negotiating the purchase of the mansion in the king's name, to be paid for from the monarch's privy purse. Ever since, Hôtel de Beauharnais has belonged to the German state and is now the official residence of the German Ambassador.

THE BATHROOM
Designed in Pompeian style,
its decorative mosaic floor illustrates
the theme of the *Rape of Europa*.
The artful interplay of mirrors creates
an illusion of endless space.

MONACO
IN MATIGNON

Hôtel de Goyon-Matignon

57 Rue de Varenne

**THE FAÇADE OVERLOOKING
THE MAIN COURTYARD**
View of the semi-circular main
entrance portal, designed
by Jean Courtonne, 1721.

Hôtel de Goyon-Matignon, nowadays the official residence of the French Prime Minister, is the most elegant mansion in the Faubourg Saint-Germain, unrivalled in its harmonious proportions and the majestic size and splendour of its gardens which were redesigned around 1889 by Achile Duchêne.

In 1721, Christian-Louis de Montmorency-Luxembourg, Prince de Tingry, Lieutenant-General of the Royal Armies and later Marshal, commissioned the architect and entrepreneur Jean Courtonne to design the mansion. Faced with spiralling costs, the Prince and Princesse de Tingry pulled out of the project and, two years later, sold the uncompleted building to Jacques Goyon de Matignon who had the fitting out and decorating of the mansion continued. Goyon de Matignon, an extremely wealthy man and much esteemed figure at Louis XV's court, built up an outstanding collection of works of art which was later added to by his son, the Duc de Valentinois.

The Goyon-Matignon residence was said to resemble a palace rather than a town house. The façade overlooking the courtyard was embellished with a profusion of sculptures, offering a foretaste of the sumptuous interiors. The large panelled reception room – known as the 'Gilt Room' – which projects into the garden has lost none of its elegance. It still boasts a marble chimney-piece surmounted by a magnificent, floral garlanded pier-glass and flanked by large panels decorated with shells and sprigs of ivy, and has overdoors painted by Nicolas Lancret.

When M. de Matignon died in 1725, he was succeeded by his son, Jacques-François, who ostentatiously bore the style and titles of his young wife, Louise-Hippolyte Grimaldi de Valentinois, heiress to the princes of Monaco: despairing at the lack of a son, Prince Antoine de Monaco had arranged for his eldest daughter to find a suitably wealthy suitor who could pay off the massive debts which he had incurred. Saint-Simon informs us that, although the sums demanded by the Prince were colossal, "Matignon, thanks to the wealth he had amassed under M. de Chamillart's ministry and by his own thrift, had more than enough to satisfy M. de Monaco's great needs". On the couple's marriage in 1715, the Valentinois dukedom and peerage had been created for Jacques-François de Matignon; henceforth, the new duke and all his descendants supplanted, both in name and in rights, the house of Grimaldi de Monaco. Nevertheless, the mansion on which the couple lavished such care retained the name of Matignon in compliance with the dying wish of the new Duc de Valentinois' father.

The Valentinois' collection of works of art was outstanding. In 1749, the author of the *Mémorial de Paris* wrote: "It would require a whole

THE GRAND STAIRCASE
Embellished with diverse ornamental marbles, its elegance derives from the harmonious proportions and sweeping banister.

| French School
LOUISE-HIPPOLYTE GRIMALDI,
PRINCESSE DE MONACO,
DUCHESSE DE VALENTINOIS

18th century, oil on copper,
47 × 39 cm (18 ½ × 15 ³⁄₈ in).

Musée national du château, Versailles.

THE YELLOW ROOM
This reception room,
with its white
and gold panelling,
opens onto the largest
private garden in Paris.

volume to describe all the splendours which decorate this palace which few in Italy could rival." In 1751, the duke and duchess were succeeded by their son, Honoré III de Matignon, Prince de Monaco, notorious for his marital tribulations since his wife publicly flaunted her affair with the Prince de Condé.

The years were tranquilly drifting by for the ageing prince when the Revolution suddenly erupted. Although Richelieu had established an alliance between France and Monaco under the terms of the Treaty of Péronne, the Legislative Assembly abolished the prince's feudal rights. His children having emigrated, Honoré III became a helpless spectator as his principality was forcibly incorporated into the French Republic. He was then arrested and held in the former Couvent des Oiseaux in Rue de Sèvres, along with the cream of Faubourg Saint-Germain society. There, on 10 Thermidor in the Year II [28 July 1794], he learned that his daughter-in-law had been executed the previous day. When the Revolutionary Tribunal had sentenced her to death, seeking to obtain one night of reprieve in order to cut off her own hair, she had declared she was pregnant. The old prince died shortly after his release from prison and, as his estate was crippled by debts, the mansion was auctioned off. It was acquired by Eleonora Sullivan, an Italian lady from Lucca, an international adventuress and mistress to several crowned heads. Since 1783, she had been living with the British spy and connoisseur art collector, Quentin Crawford, who had grown fabulously rich in Manila. The couple, who sprang straight from the pages of some romantic novel, had helped Axel de Fersen prepare the attempted flight of the French royal family on 20 June 1791, and had re-emerged in Paris during the Consulate thanks to the friendly — and self-interested — offices of Talleyrand who was himself in debt to the millionaire Crawford. Mme Sullivan held lavish receptions in Rue de Varenne and, displaying impeccable taste, furnished the mansion in unprecedented luxury. In 1808, Talleyrand became the owner of the property and in turn organized extravagant revelries right up to the dying days of the Empire, before handing the mansion over to the State Property Department. The premises were occupied by successive members of the Orléans family and subsequently used for a variety of purposes. In 1935, Hôtel de Matignon became the official residence of the Président du Conseil, or French Prime Minister.

THE GRAND RECEPTION ROOM
A view of the lavish gilding, overdoors, highlighted decors, painted panels and sky-blue ceiling quartered by a cross motif.

A MECCA OF THE ARTS AND LITERATURE

Hôtel Peyrenc de Moras, or Biron

77 Rue de Varenne

THE FAÇADE OVERLOOKING THE GARDEN
Built by Jacques-Ange Gabriel
and Aubert around 1727.

Unfortunately, all that remains of this magnificent mansion, once home to such leading figures as the Duchesse du Maine or the sculptor Rodin, are the exteriors and the recently restored panelling in the reception room. On the other hand, it is one of the rare Parisian *hôtels* which has conserved its extensive gardens virtually intact.

In 1727, Abraham Peyrenc de Moras, a financier of international repute who had grown wealthy in Paris and London from Law's credit system, purchased a large plot of waste land in the Faubourg Saint-Germain. Born Abraham Perrin, the son of a humble wig-maker in Le Vigan, no sooner had he made his fortune than he sought to add a veneer of nobility to his family name by changing it to 'Peyrenc' and appending the aristocratic suffix 'de Moras' – a seigniorial domain which he had acquired.

Having purchased the office of *maître des requêtes* – an advisory post at the Council of State – the financier then set out to build a mansion befitting his massive and rapidly-earned fortune. He commissioned the fashionable architect Jacques-Ange Gabriel to draw up plans for the new residence and Aubert to supervise the work. Peyrenc de Moras' fabulous wealth enabled him to hire the most famous artists. According to contemporary documents, "the large reception room, panelled with

sea-green painted oak pilasters, had four pier-glasses, a pair of which were placed above the chimney-piece and the console opposite, and two others facing the casement windows giving onto the garden". Over the doors and closets, four paintings by Lemoyne symbolized the various times of day: morning, with *Aurora Carrying Off Cephalus*; noon, with *Venus and the Graces Showing Cupid the Ardour of his Arrows*; and evening and night illustrated by a *Diana Returning from the Hunt*, and *Diana and Endymion*. The decor included overdoors and painted panelling by Coypel and Nicolas Pineau.

The work was completed in 1730 and Peyrenc de Moras took up residence, only to die two years later. His widow acquired further parcels of land and the garden was extended as far as Rue de Babylone, creating a majestic property. And it was indeed to a royal princess, the Duchesse du Maine, Anne-Louise-Bénédicte de Bourbon-Condé (granddaughter of 'the Great Condé' and widow of the son of Louis XIV and Mme de Montespan) that Mme Peyrenc de Moras rented the spanking new premises in 1736.

Since 1692, the Duchesse du Maine had presided over a sort of literary court at the Château de Sceaux where her entourage used to compose poems for her and declaim odes, epigrams, charades and madrigals, and where she had commissioned the building of a small theatre. Cardinal Dubois, convinced that he had detected the duchess's hand – she was forever embroiled in some scheme or other – in a murky plot against the Regent – the so-called Cellamare conspiracy, after the name of the Spanish Ambassador – had ordered her arrest and had her incarcerated in the castle at Dijon. When Louis XV came to the throne, she returned to Sceaux and resumed her literary activities. The protection she offered Voltaire and several other writers established her well-deserved reputation as a patroness and champion of the arts and literature. Accordingly, from 1736, when she took up residence in her mansion in Rue de Varenne in Paris, she continued to organize artistic gatherings there until her death in 1753 at the age of seventy-seven. At that point, the Peyrenc de Moras heirs sold the family property, for an extremely high price, to Antoine-Louis de Gontaut-Biron, Colonel of the French Guards, Marshal and Peer of France, and husband of Mlle de La Rochefoucauld de Roye. The Maréchal and Maréchale de Biron had the gardens – more remarkable for their horticultural variety than for their layout – redesigned. The marshal proudly doubled the number of flower-beds and box edgings, and commissioned a large central basin and ornamental fountain with a group of sculpted children representing the four seasons. He then incorporated a new parcel

THE FIRST OVAL RECEPTION ROOM
The original natural wood panelling
has been re-installed
in the Duchesse du Maine's
reception room,
but not the overdoors
by Coypel.

| François de Troy
**ANNE-LOUISE-BÉNÉDICTE
DE BOURBON-CONDÉ,
DUCHESSE DU MAINE
(PRESUMED PORTRAIT)**
1694, oil on canvas,
22 × 17 cm (8 ⅝ × 6 ⅝ in).
Musée des Beaux-Arts, Orléans.

THE SECOND OVAL RECEPTION ROOM
This room has also
had its original decor restored.

of land into the property, laying out terraced groves and trellises and a Chinese pavilion and marquee for musical performances. His grandiose receptions were the talk of the town. When the Maréchal de Biron died in 1788, the mansion was jointly inherited by his wife and his handsome son, 'Beau' Lauzun, who, after having fought with conspicuous gallantry during the American War of Independence, had attempted to seduce Marie-Antoinette at court. The Revolution dealt a ruthless blow to the owners of Hôtel de Biron. Lauzun, who had become Duc de Biron and was a close friend of the Duc d'Orléans, was guillotined in December 1793 while his unfortunate wife, née Amélie de Boufflers and highly esteemed for her philanthropic activities, found herself, owing to a mix-up over names, on the way to the scaffold in the same tumbrel as her mother-in-law, the Maréchale.

After the Terror, the extensive property was inherited by the Duc de Béthune-Charrost. In Thermidor in the Year V [late July 1797], during the Directory, the duke began to rent out the old Rue de Varenne mansion to a private company which organized popular balls. The pages of a contemporary gazette, *Les petites annonces et avis divers*, offer a glimpse of the range of amusements offered: these included balls with

THE FAÇADE AND GARDEN

The Duc de Biron's landscaped
garden with its arbours
and bowers, garlands
of honeysuckle, melonbeds
and fountain basins was converted
into an amusement park
under the Directory.

accompanying orchestra, concerts, illuminations, displays of fireworks by Ruggieri or acrobatics by Franconi, balloon ascents by the Blanchards, and parachute jumps by the Garnerin brothers (28 August 1797). The old Duc de Béthune-Charrost, who had continued to reside in the mansion, died there in 1800.

After having housed the Papal Nuncio Caprara and then the Russian Ambassador, from 1820 the premises were occupied by a boarding-school for young aristocratic ladies run by Sophie Barrat and nuns from the Sacré-Cœur congregation. The school directors had some of the interior decors removed on the pretext that certain painted motifs might distract their pupils' attention.

When the congregation was dissolved in 1904, the building was used as a municipal school before being split up into apartments. Among the residents were the dancer, Isadora Duncan, writers like Rainer Maria Rilke and artists such as the sculptor Rodin. It was thanks to the latter that the mansion was saved. In 1916, Rodin signed an agreement stipulating that he would bequeath all his works to the state on condition that they remained in the Hôtel Peyrenc de Moras, or Biron. Today, the Rodin Museum, standing amidst its magnificent gardens, attracts countless visitors who flock to admire the sculptor's work.

THE SOUTH FAÇADE OVERLOOKING THE GARDEN
Overhanging a huge balcony, the ornamental pediment is decorated with a *Flora* accompanied by Cupids.

3. Other Districts of Paris

GENTLE CARIBBEAN BREEZES

Hôtel de Bourrienne

58 Rue d'Hauteville

Andrea Appiani |
MADAME HAMELIN
1798, oil on canvas,
70 × 55 cm (27 ⅝ × 21 ⅝ in).
Musée Carnavalet, Paris.

Pages 180 and 181 |
THE BEDCHAMBER
The Empire style ceiling decoration
is by Étienne-Chérubin Leconte.

The elegant Rue d'Hauteville, which runs from the 'grands boulevards' to the church of Saint-Vincent-de-Paul, was parcelled out into plots late in the reign of Louis XVI. Before being acquired by the Bourrienne family during the Consulate, the mansion which bears their name had already had several owners in the twelve years since it had been built. It actually dates from just before the Revolution, although the interior decoration was not completed until the Directory and is stylistically typical of the latter period.

In March 1792, when France declared war on the coalition states – a seemingly inappropriate moment to invest in real estate – Mme Lormier-Lagrave purchased the mansion at 58 Rue d'Hauteville. She was a resolute woman, and was determined not to go back to her home in Saint-Domingue (present-day Haiti). Moreover, she was well connected in leading political circles. This Creole lady was separated from her husband, an extremely wealthy planter; he had returned to Saint-Domingue on business but was drowned there in 1794, attempting to flee the insurrection on the island. Citizeness Lormier-Lagrave lived in the Rue d'Hauteville mansion with her daughter Jeanne-Geneviève, known as Fortunée, born in Saint-Domingue in 1776 following an adulterous affair. Among the influential relations whom she received there was Fouché, member of the National Convention and future Imperial Minister of Police, who apparently protected the two women during the Terror. In July 1792, the attractive daughter, Fortunée Lormier-Lagrave, had married Romain Hamelin, grandson of a farmer-general and himself involved – like several others – in the provision of military supplies and services, an activity which offered endless opportunities to embezzle public funds. Romain Hamelin, accompanied by his wife, had followed Napoleon on the latter's Italian campaigns. In Milan, Mme Hamelin had struck up a friendship with another Creole lady, citizeness Bonaparte, the future Empress Joséphine. Appiani's famous portrait of her dates from this period; Joséphine herself and Laure Regnaud de Saint-Jean d'Angely also posed for the painter.

Since her father's accidental death Mme Hamelin had become the legal owner of the mansion in Rue d'Hauteville although her visits there were sporadic. Her mother was left to while away the hours in endless games of *trente-et-un* [a card game in which one must mark 31 points with three cards to win], hoping to restore a fortune that had been much diminished by the pillaging of the family plantations. Endowed with sparkling wit and great natural charm, Fortunée became a fashionable celebrity during the Directory. Along with her husband, she took up residence in a nearby town house on the corner of Boulevard des

**THE FAÇADE OVERLOOKING
THE GARDEN**

Embellished
with four allegorical
representations
of the goddess *Fame*.
The two central figures bear
wreaths while the other two
are shown with a palm leaf
and a wreath. The wings
and upper section above
the cornice are later additions.

THE BEDCHAMBER
Detail of a panel featuring
arabesques and an amphora.

Italiens and Rue Taitbout and then moved to Rue Chauchat. When she returned to Rue d'Hauteville in 1798, it was to inform her mother that she wished to sell the mansion. The property was acquired by one of her mother's relatives and then both mansion and garden were sold three years later to Antoine Fauvelet, Comte de Bourrienne. Almost immediately after this the count, a former schoolfellow and private secretary of Bonaparte, was implicated in an affair involving the embezzlement of military supplies and was packed off to (gilded) exile in Hamburg where, in 1804, he was appointed chargé d'affaires and acted as French Ambassador.

In 1813, Bourrienne was officially posted back to Paris, rejoining his wife and daughters who had continued to live and socialize in the capital. On his return, the never-ending round of receptions grew even more lavish – thanks to the money from bribes taken while pursuing his lofty diplomatic functions – and continued right up to, and during, the Restoration. Far from sharing the virtues of the faithful Achates, this former friend of Bonaparte had unhesitatingly swapped allegiance on the return of the Bourbons. He played host to many friends, including Mme Hamelin. The mansion in which, as a sensible young girl living with a wayward mother, she had survived the dark days of the

Terror was still fresh in her memory. Nothing had changed. The passage-way opening onto an interior courtyard, separated from the street by some nondescript buildings, still led to the house. The façade over-looking the superb landscaped garden still boasted its four allegorical *Fames* with their wreaths and palm leaves. The marvellous interior still retained its elegant decor of painted panelling and moulding which Mme Lormier-Lagrave, lavish with her daughter's money, had commis-sioned from fashionable artists during the Revolution. The paintwork in the large reception room had lost none of its green and yellow lustre, and the overdoors and monochrome panels were still studded with little mythological scenes. The parquet flooring was a majestic, harmo-nious blend of precious woods – rosewood, citron wood and maho-gany – while the ceilings – notably the canopied ceiling in the recep-tion room and the sky-blue ceiling in the dining room – conjured up memories of gently wafting Caribbean breezes.

In 1824, the Bourriennes were forced to leave the mansion that held so many fond memories. Since then, although there have been many different owners, they have all endeavoured, despite every obstacle, to preserve intact this little paradise of greenery tucked away in the heart of bustling Paris.

A Royal Favourite

Hôtel Benoît de Saint-Paulle

30 Rue du Faubourg-Poissonnière

François Boucher |
Marie-Louise O'Morphy
1757, oil on canvas,
59 × 73 cm (23 $^1/_4$ × 28 $^3/_4$ in).
Alte Pinakothek, Munich.

As a result of property speculation, Claude-Martin Goupy, a contractor for the Bâtiments du Roi [responsible for the royal buildings], had acquired several parcels of land in the Chaussée de la Nouvelle-France district, the present-day Faubourg Poissonnière. Works were carried out to make the plots suitable for building and the land was then sold to M. Benoît de Sainte-Paulle who wished to build a mansion on the site. As the costs incurred were far larger than initially estimated, M. de Sainte-Paulle, who had commissioned the work in 1780, sold the still-uncompleted property to the wealthy financier François-Nicolas Lenormand de Flaghac and his wife, née Marie-Louise O'Morphy, a celebrated Parisian society figure since 1753.

"On 15 May 1753," relates the Duc de Croy, "court and city were buzzing with two rumours." One rumour concerned the disastrous expulsion of the Paris Parlement to Pontoise, the other involved an attractive girl who had, for several months, been Louis XV's mistress. The girl, it was said, was gaining in the monarch's favour at the expense of Mme de Pompadour who found the situation disturbing, "particularly at a time when the marquise was thinking of allying with the 'devout' party at court to maintain spiritual influence over the king, just as Mme de Maintenon had done in the past". Before all this took place, however, the attractive lady in question, the future Mme Lenormand de Flaghac, already had a long history of amorous adventures behind her...

Marie-Louise O'Morphy was the eldest of five daughters of a more or less indigent Irish gentleman forced to live by his wits. Accordingly, the girls had to seek support elsewhere and posed for various artists, notably Boucher, of whom Marie-Louise was the favourite model.

Pages 188 and 189
**THE FAÇADE OVERLOOKING
THE MAIN COURTYARD**
The mansion was built
by Samson-Nicolas Lenoir in 1773.

Attributed to Louis-Michel Van Loo
PORTRAIT OF LOUIS XV
1760, oil on canvas,
22 × 18 cm (8 ⅝ × 7 ⅛ in).
Musée national du château, Versailles.

When barely fourteen years old, she had caught the eye of Lebel, whose task was to scout for potential candidates for Louis XV's extra-marital diversions. The mouth-watering young creature had "an ample bosom" and was "well developed" for her age. It was rumoured in Versailles that Boucher had used her as a model in his painting *Saint John the Baptist Preaching in the Wilderness*, which nowadays hangs in St Louis' church in that town. Having successfully appealed to the royal taste, she was initially provided with accommodation at Versailles and then in a small house in the Deer Park. She bore the king a daughter in 1754, but the monarch realized that she did not have the makings of a royal favourite as she lacked finesse and tact. Under the name of Louise Morphy de Boisfailly, he married her off to an Auvergnat gentleman and then subsequently to François-Nicolas Lenormand de Flaghac.

Although merely a passing favourite, the lady who became known as 'la Morphise' had nevertheless managed to make the most of her short-lived privilege. She had had the aristocratic origins of her family officially recognized and had then persuaded Lenormand to buy Hôtel Benoît de Sainte-Paulle in Rue du Faubourg-Poissonnière. No sooner had the couple moved in than the husband died. La Morphise drew heavily on her children's inheritance to convert the mansion to her own convenience, renting out part of the premises to her new lover, Valdec de Lessart, so that they could live together as man and wife under the same roof.

The mansion, as it then stood, included a building giving onto the street, with a carriage entrance opening into a large courtyard. It was flanked on either side by wings with Mansart roofs, while the main building, at the far end of the courtyard, consisted of a five-bay pavilion with a semi-basement floor, ground floor, square first storey and an attic storey with a flat roof. To the rear, a huge garden stretched as far as the present-day Rue d'Hauteville. It was one of the finest town gardens in the district, stamped with the Italianate hallmark of Lenoir who had supervized the initial stage of work on the mansion. On either side of the central basin, two parallel alleys were lined with fragrant lime trees. At the end of the garden stood a large statue of Flora and, at its foot, a series of small vases placed on stone plinths. The central alley leading back towards the house culminated in a little bower with benches set around a piece of classical statuary. La Morphise was fond of such garden spaces formed by trellises and hedges, occasionally covered, where refreshments could be served, or music enjoyed, and which were ideal for discreet flirtation. The combination of different alleys and viewpoints magnified the overall impression of space.

Having escaped the guillotine, Mme Lenormand de Flaghac managed to get her fine Rue du Faubourg-Poissonnière mansion back; but then, wishing to retire to her country seat of Château de Soisy near Étioles, she finally decided to part with it. In the 19th century, although the property changed hands several times, both mansion and garden remained intact. After 1914, interior office space was laid out, new floors were added without any proper planning, the plot was divided up, and all sorts of damage was perpetrated. Yet both the façade overlooking the courtyard and the wings at right angles to it have withstood the ravages of time and the main building still boasts its fine capitals and doors.

REAR VIEW OF THE FAÇADE GIVING ONTO THE STREET
The courtyard has retained many of its original decorative features.

Games of Love and Chance

Hôtel d'Augny

6 Rue Drouot

| Jean-Louis Boyer
Mlle Saulnier, wife of the Marquis de Livry
C. 1785, patinated plaster, height 65 cm (25 5/8 in).
Private collection, Paris.

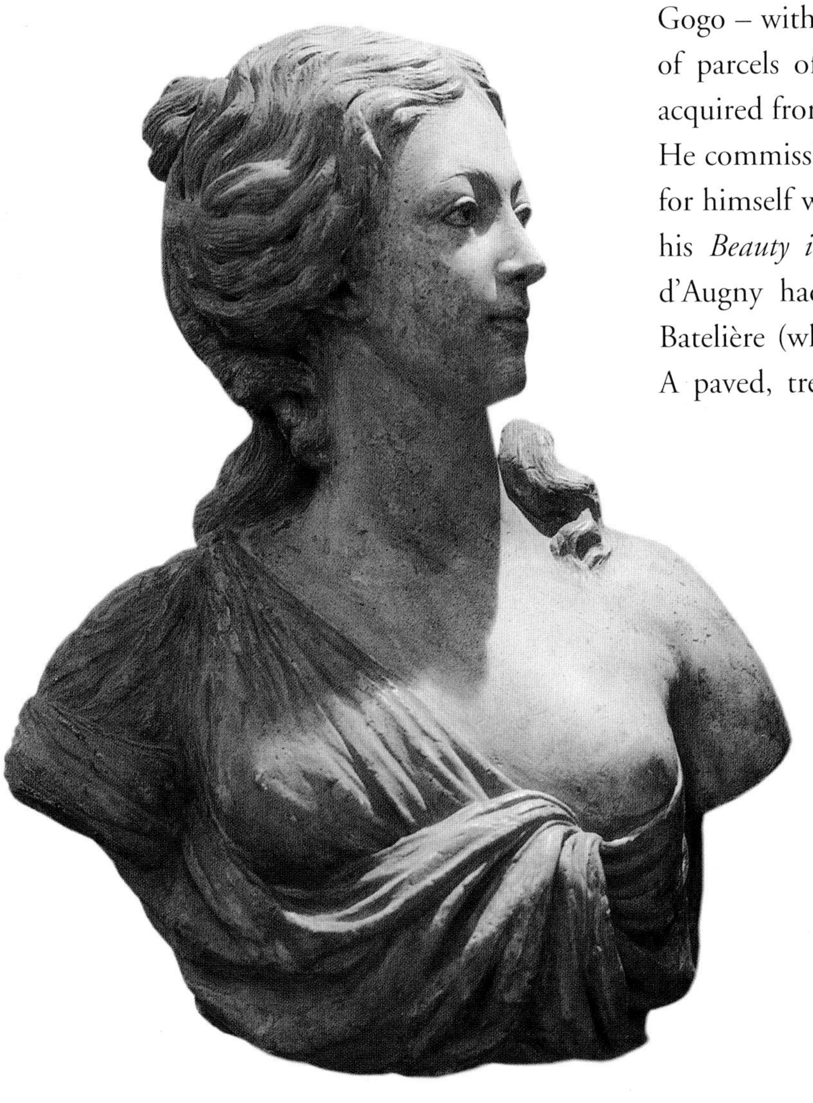

Hôtel d'Augny – occasionally spelled Daugny or d'Ogny – was built in the mid-18th century, and became a celebrated libertine rendezvous at a time when the court at Versailles set the pace in rakish living. The Grange-Batelière district, where countryside met town, lay just beyond the boulevards. Greenery still prevailed there when, in a flurry of speculative property deals, great aristocrats, financiers and courtesans set about building Neo-Classical mansions with landscaped gardens. In 1750, in order to make way for an elegant mansion, the wealthy Baron d'Augny, himself son of a farmer-general and at the time totally infatuated with an actress, Mlle Beaumenard – known as Gogo – with whom he wished to set up house, had cleared a number of parcels of land bordering the 'grands boulevards' which he had acquired from various individual sellers.

He commissioned a leading architect, Briseux, who had made a name for himself with his *Treatise on the Art of Building Country Houses* and his *Beauty in Architecture.* Like many mansions in the area, Hôtel d'Augny had a monumental carriage entrance onto Rue Grange-Batelière (which nowadays forms the lower stretch of Rue Drouot). A paved, tree-lined passageway led to the main courtyard and the

The stairwell
Hôtel d'Augny's monumental staircase was designed during the Empire for the lavish receptions held by the Marquis de Livry.

house itself. On either side of the main section of the mansion, Briseux designed other buildings which opened onto smaller courtyards and were intended to house the kitchens and servants' quarters and to accommodate the stables and coach houses. The central building, a pioneering example of the Neo-Classical style which would soon sweep through the district, was built on two storeys with attic rooms. On the other side, to the east, lay a huge garden, skirted by present-day Rue du Faubourg-Montmartre. Here, Baron d'Augny laid out an indoor riding-school, marble baths, a poultry yard and a dairy.

For the interior decoration, d'Augny, himself a reputed connoisseur, commissioned the talented Pineau to carve the reception room sculptures, while the painted ceilings, pier panels and overdoors were attributed by the author of *Le voyageur pittoresque*, written in 1765, to Boucher, Pierre, Huilliot and Le Lorrain.

On the outbreak of the Revolution, Baron d'Augny took the precaution of moving out of Paris and then emigrated, following the example of his principal tenant, Comte de Mercy-Argenteau, Empress Maria Theresa's celebrated ambassador at the French court.

During the Directory, new tenants in Hôtel d'Augny, the Marquis and Marquise de Livry, set up the 'Club des Étrangers' ('The Foreigners' Club'), the most famous gambling club in Europe. The original club had been founded just before the Revolution by Livry and his boon companion Vicomte de Castellane in the Winter Vauxhall in Rue de Chartres-Saint-Honoré and had then moved to Rue du Mail in 1791. Livry acted as the grand impresario of fashionable entertainment for the Parisian social set. With the help of his wife, former prima ballerina at the Opéra, he also organized spectacular balls at Hôtel d'Augny. An account of such evenings can be read in the pages of *Paris et ses modes*: "Guests used to dine in six or eight reception rooms and the celebrated caterers Robert and Lointier would take turns at planning the menus. Everyone wore masks, whether dining, dancing or gambling... On the first few occasions, splendid, copious fare was elegantly served up on silver and silver-gilt dishes; everything was available for the mere asking. Some of the guests, however, used to help themselves to more than jellies or ices; shielded from public disgrace or censure behind their masks and costumes, they would pocket the expensive cutlery as well. The organizers cancelled the suppers, restricting the attractions to ices, dancing and gambling. And now even masked gambling is no longer permitted."

Masked balls were subsequently banned when one of Joséphine's ladies-in-waiting, taking advantage of her disguise, gambled and lost

THE GARDEN FAÇADE

The gardens were formerly very extensive, stretching as far as the present-day Rue du Faubourg-Poissonnière. All that remains of the original mansion are the façades.

such a large amount of money that she was dismissed from her post and drummed out of court at the Tuileries. Following this scandal, Hôtel d'Augny, the popularity of which was already on the wane, was put under close surveillance. Napoleon only authorized the organizers to pursue their gambling activities on condition that the Club des Étrangers reverted to its original vocation and catered exclusively for wealthy foreign visitors to Paris.

After 1798, the mansion was taken over from Master Perrin, the Lottery Administrator, by one of Livry's friends, Jean-Joseph Bernard, who had been Paris Gaming Tax Collector since 1813. From 1829, its fortunes were triumphantly revived thanks to Vicomte Aguado, a Spanish gentleman born in Seville, who had served as an officer under Napoleon and had been Maréchal Soult's aide-de-camp. The viscount had amassed a huge fortune as a result of his business activities and when he was appointed banker to the Spanish court he proved himself to be a generous patron of the arts. A passionate opera-lover, he helped launch the composer Rossini in Paris and installed the old Hôtel d'Augny to his own taste in a sumptuous, somewhat flashy style which the mansion has definitively lost since the Town Hall of the 9th arrondissement of Paris was installed in the premises in 1849.

**THE FAÇADE OVERLOOKING
THE MAIN COURTYARD**

Built between 1748 and 1752
to designs by Charles-Étienne Briseux.
The two wings date from 1870.

THE DOOMED PRINCESS

Hôtel de Lamballe

17 Rue d'Ankara

THE FAÇADE OVERLOOKING THE GARDEN
The façade, with its large
twin-staircased balcony, looks out
onto the Seine. The main building
has monumental Doric pilasters
and a straight-fronted attic storey.
The mansion was designed
by an unknown architect during
Louis XVI's reign.

Joseph-Siffrein Duplessis |
MARIE-THÉRÈSE DE SAVOIE-CARIGNAN,
PRINCESSE DE LAMBALLE
N.d., oil on canvas,
81 × 65 cm (31 $^7/_8$ × 25 $^5/_8$ in).
Musées de la Cour d'Or, Metz.

Between the heights of Chaillot and the Seine, halfway up the slope leading to Passy, stretched a marvellous wooded park. It was here that the owners, the Princesse de Lamballe and her father-in-law, the Duc de Penthièvre, posed for the portrait painter Jean-Baptiste Charpentier. The melancholy princess loved to retire to her majestic domain and the mansion set in its grounds. A young widow, to whom love had been unkind, she was destined to die a horrible death in the courtyard of La Force prison during the September massacres in 1792.

The Duc de Lauzun, a legendary rake in true Regency fashion, had resided in the mansion from 1700. But it was above all his wife who lived there. Among her notable guests were her brother-in-law, the famous memorialist Saint-Simon, and his sister, Mme de Saint-Simon, together with the Duchesse de Bourgogne, for whom she held lavish receptions, and also Mme Law. The Duchesse de Lauzun lived in the mansion until 1734 and then sold it to another grand lady, the Marquise de Saissac, whose husband was a notorious card-sharp. It was eventually inherited by the Duc de Luynes in 1775.

Finally, the property was coveted, and acquired, by a prince of the blood, the amiable Duc de Penthièvre, grandson of Louis XIV and Mme de Montespan. Although there is no record of the alterations or embellishments he introduced, it is certain that the duke, reputed to be the wealthiest gentleman in France, was determined that the estate, which he had earmarked for the Princesse de Lamballe, would be a fitting jewel for his beloved daughter-in-law. Indeed, the Duc de Penthièvre remained extremely close to the young woman who had been his son's wife for no more than a few brief months: the Prince de Lamballe had met an early death at the age of 20 in 1768.

In February 1783, when Marie-Thérèse de Savoie-Carignan, Princesse de Lamballe, took possession of her new residence, nestling amidst large trees planted in the days of the Sun King and with its magnificent, clear, sweeping view out over the Seine, she had been Superintendent of the Queen's Household for nine years. A stickler for etiquette, she did not readily follow Marie-Antoinette and her entourage who all too often forsook the stilted palace atmosphere of Versailles for the pleasures of the hamlet at Trianon. When she could free herself from court duties, she would withdraw to her estate in Passy. The garden communicated directly with her father-in-law's neighbouring mansion via a gate onto Rue Raynouard, not far from present-day Rue d'Ankara, where two charming pavilions stood at the entrance to the park.

The façade of Hôtel de Lamballe overlooking the courtyard still

consists of a central section with three bays standing beneath a large curved pediment. The ground floor boasts fine arched arcades, separated by grooved stonework, above which the three first-floor windows open. The base of the roof is crowned by a balustrade extending towards the wings. The façade overlooking the garden and the Seine opens onto a large balcony with a horseshoe-shaped staircase. Beneath this balcony, a cool spot had been laid out, a rustic grotto with a small basin designed to fill with spring water from the hillside. It was in this luxurious retreat that the royal superindent was paid the honour of a visit from Madame Élisabeth, Louis XVI's sister, and from the queen herself who, moreover, loved to stay at her own neighbouring Château de La Muette in Passy.

On the outbeak of the Revolution, the foreign-born Princesse de Lamballe had good reasons to emigrate and return to the court of Turin. And this she did when the royal family, also attempting to flee, were arrested at Varennes on 21 June 1791. She made her way to London and then to Aachen where, prompted by some fatal premonition, she drew up her will. At Marie-Antoinette's request, she came back to Paris in the winter of 1791-1792. At the Tuileries, she resumed her prerogatives as Superintendent of the Queen's Household and was also involved in the 'Austrian committee', in actual fact counter-revolutionary meetings which she organized with the assent of Marie-Antoinette. On 10 August 1792, she was in the company of the royal family when, along with the queen's 'ladies', she was arrested on the suspicion of having abetted secret communications between the deposed monarchs and their foreign and émigré allies and was eventually incarcerated in La Force prison. On 2 September, as massacres were breaking out in other Parisian prisons – panic had gripped the city since news had arrived of foreign armies at the frontiers – she was hauled before a makeshift popular tribunal to explain her presence at La Force. The princess, notoriously loyal to the royal family, could offer no defence. The order "Release the lady!" was given and she was dragged by two henchmen into the prison courtyard towards the exit. Suddenly abandoned by her 'guards' to the mercy of a drunken crowd, she was insulted, attacked and murdered. The unfortunate woman's headless body was stripped, dragged in the dirt and mutilated. Her head was paraded through the streets of Paris to the Temple where the royal family were interned. Although Marie-Antoinette did not actually witness the horrible spectacle enacted beneath her prison windows, it was impossible to conceal from her the violent death of the woman who had remained her most faithful companion right up to the ultimate catastrophe.

The very next day, Mme de Lamballe's mansion in Passy was sealed up by the authorities. Initially seized as émigré property, in May 1796 it was the subject of an agreement between the French Republic and the King of Sardinia; finally, in January 1797, it was restored to Charles-Emmanuel de Savoie-Carignan, the Princesse de Lamballe's nephew and heir who immediately sold it to the banker Baguenault, the latter remaining its owner until 1845. Subsequently, the estate accommodated a Mental Hospital run by Doctor Esprit Blanche. He was succeeded by his son, Émile Blanche, in 1852. Among the patients were Gérard de Nerval – who was treated there on two occasions – Gounod and Maupassant, the latter dying on the premises in 1893. At the beginning of the century, the heirs split the vast property up into separate lots divided by two avenues. Hidden away behind high walls, the mansion, along with a shrunken vestige of the former gardens, still stands today, housing the Turkish Embassy.

DETAIL OF THE STAIRCASE
Designed in the form of a horseshoe, it frames the entrance to a grotto containing a small basin into which water from the Passy springs used to flow.

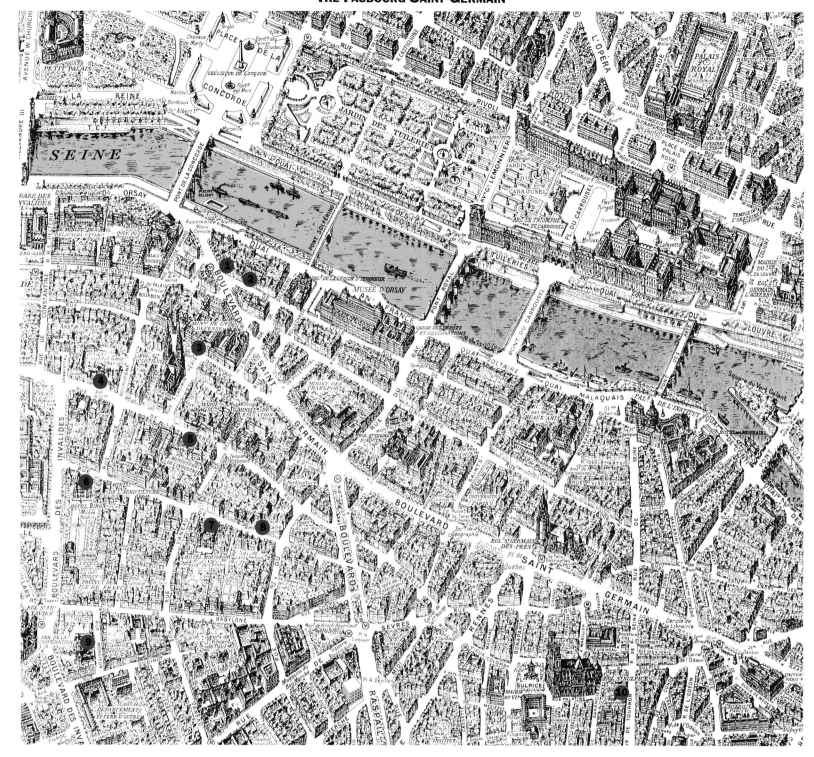

1 **HÔTEL DE SEIGNELAY**
80 Rue de Lille
75007 Paris

2 **HÔTEL DE BEAUHARNAIS**
78 Rue de Lille
75007 Paris

3 **HÔTEL DE BRIENNE**
14 Rue Saint-Dominique
75007 Paris

4 **HÔTEL DE NOIRMOUTIER**
138 Rue de Grenelle
75007 Paris

5 **HÔTEL DE ROTHELIN-CHAROLAIS**
101 Rue de Grenelle
75007 Paris

6 **HÔTEL PEYRENC DE MORAS, OU BIRON ***
77 Rue de Varenne
75007 Paris

7 **HÔTEL DE GOYON-MATIGNON**
57 Rue de Varenne
75007 Paris

8 **HÔTEL DE GALLIFET**
50 Rue de Varenne
75007 Paris

9 **HÔTEL DE BOURBON-CONDÉ**
12 Rue Monsieur
75007 Paris

10 **HÔTEL D'ENTRAGUES**
12 Rue de Tournon
75006 Paris

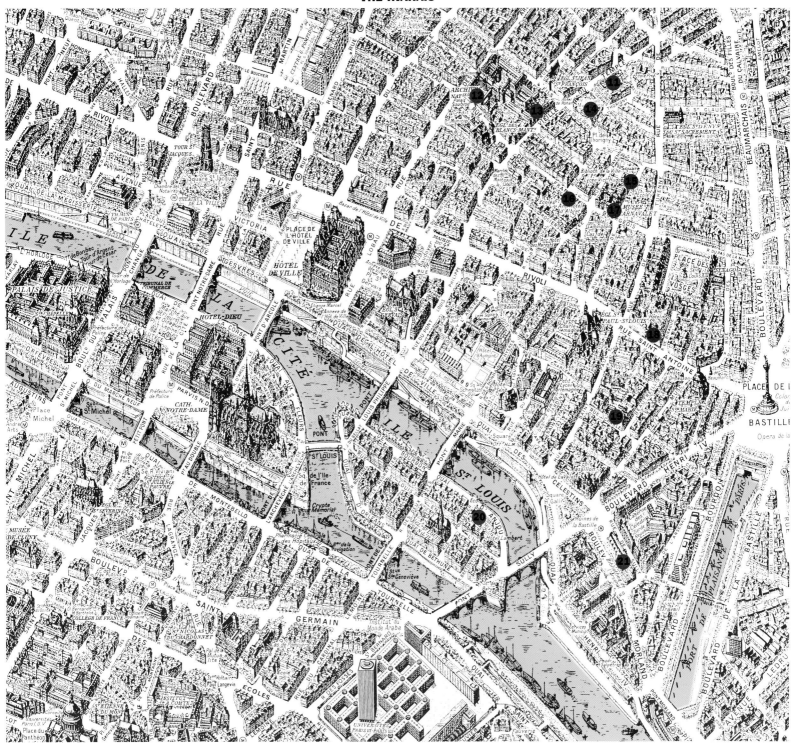

11 **HÔTEL MÉGRET DE SÉRILLY**
106 Rue Vieille-du-Temple
75003 Paris

12 **HÔTEL DE SOUBISE** *
60 Rue des Francs-Bourgeois
75003 Paris

13 **HÔTEL DE ROHAN-STRASBOURG** *
87 Rue Vieille-du-Temple
75003 Paris

14 **HÔTEL AUBERT DE FONTENAY** *
5 Rue de Thorigny
75003 Paris

15 **HÔTEL LE PELETIER**
DE SAINT-FARGEAU *
29 Rue de Sévigné
75003 Paris

16 **HÔTEL D'ALBRET**
31 Rue des Francs-Bourgeois
75003 Paris

17 **HÔTEL CARNAVALET** *
23 Rue de Sévigné
75003 Paris

18 **HÔTEL DE SULLY** *
62 Rue Saint-Antoine
75003 Paris

19 **HÔTEL DE BRINVILLIERS**
12 Rue Charles-V
75004 Paris

20 **HÔTEL DE LAUZUN** *
17 Quai d'Anjou
75004 Paris

21 **PAVILLON DE L'ARSENAL** *
1 and 3 Rue de Sully
75004 Paris

* Mansions either permanently open to the public or offering guided visits on request.

MAP **205**

BIBLIOGRAPHY

J.-P. BABELON, *Demeures parisiennes sous Henri IV et Louis XIII*, Paris, Hazan, 1991.

J.-F. BLONDEL, *L'architecture française*, Paris, 1752-1756, 6 vols.

G. BRICE, *Description de Paris*, Paris, 1752, (9th ed.), 4 vols.

Y. CHRIST, J. DE SACY, P. SIGURET, *Le faubourg Saint-Germain*, Paris, Henri Veyrier, 1985.

F. CONTET, *Les vieux hôtels de Paris*, Paris, Contet, 1908-1937, 22 vols.

M. DUMOLIN, *Études de topographie parisienne*, Paris, 1929-1931, 3 vols.

M. FLEURY, A. ERLANDE-BRANDENBURG, J.-P. BABELON, *Paris monumental*, Paris, Flammarion, 1974.

M. GALLET, *Demeures parisiennes, l'époque de Louis XVI*, Paris, Le Temps, 1964.

L. HAUTECŒUR, *Histoire de l'architecture classique en France*, Paris, A. and J. Picard, 1963-1967, 6 vols.

J. HILLAIRET, *Dictionnaire historique des rues de Paris*, Paris, 1963, 2 vols.

E. KAUFMANN, *L'architecture au siècle des lumières*, Paris, Julliard, 1963.

J. C. KRAFFT, N. RANSONNETTE, *Plans, coupes et élévations des plus belles maisons et des hôtels construits à Paris et dans les environs entre 1771 et 1802*, Paris, éd. UHL, Nördlingen (GFR), 1992.

C. LEFEUVE, *Les anciennes maisons de Paris, sous Napoléon III*, Paris-Brussels, 1873.

C. DE MONTCLOS, *La mémoire des ruines, anthologie des monuments disparus en France*, Paris, Mengès, 1992.

J.-M. PÉROUSE DE MONTCLOS, *Histoire de l'architecture française de la Renaissance à la Révolution*, Paris, Mengès, 1989.

G. PILLEMENT, *Destruction de Paris*, Paris, Grasset, 1944.

B. PONS, *French Period Rooms 1650-1800*, Dijon, Faton, 1995.

L.-V. THIERY, *Guide des amateurs et des étrangers à Paris*, Paris, 1787, 2 vols.

Exhibition Catalogues

Alexandre-Théodore Brongniart, Paris, Musée Carnavalet, 1986.

Le faubourg Poissonnière, architecture, élégance et décor, Paris, Délégation à l'action artistique de la Ville de Paris, 1986.

Le faubourg Saint-Germain, la rue de l'Université, Paris, Institut Néerlandais, 1987.

Le faubourg Saint-Germain, la rue de Varenne, Paris, Musée Rodin, 1981.

Le faubourg Saint-Germain, la rue du Bac, Paris, Délégation à l'action artistique de la Ville de Paris, 1990.

Le faubourg Saint-Germain, la rue Saint-Dominique, Hôtels et amateurs, Paris, Musée Rodin, 1984.

Le faubourg Saint-Germain, le quai Voltaire, Paris, Délégation à l'action artistique de la Ville de Paris, 1990.

L'île Saint-Louis, hôtel de Lauzun, Paris, Délégation à l'action artistique de la Ville de Paris, 1997.

Le Marais, mythe et réalité, edited by J.-P. BABELON, Hôtel Sully, Paris, 1987.

La rue des Francs-Bourgeois au Marais, Paris, Délégation à l'action artistique de la Ville de Paris, 1992.

La rue de Lille, l'hôtel de Salm, Paris, Institut Néerlandais, 1983.

ACKNOWLEDGEMENTS

Éditions Pierre Terrail would like to thank the following, who have all contributed to the publication of this book: M. Von Mettenheim, M. Lorig (Embassy of the Federal Republic of Germany); M. Bleda (Turkish Embassy); M. Jenn, M. Mourlon, Mme Lalaut (Archives nationales); M. Philippot (Association familiale ménagère); Mme Michèle (Bibliothèque nationale de France); M. Robert, M. Lasserre (Bureau de la gestion des meubles et du matériel): M. Galey, Mme Laidaoui (Caisse nationale des monuments historiques et des sites); M. Gautier, Mme Deleau (Direction des affaires culturelles de la Ville de Paris); Mlle Chirac (Palais de l'Élysée); M. Corsi, Mme Rebecchini (Italian Cultural Institute); M. Jaymes, M. Kaspereit (Mairie du 9th Arrondissement): M. Mignot (ministère de l'Éducation nationale); M. Leri, Mme Nouri, Mme Stierle (musée Carnavalet); M. Chauvet, Mme Houel (musée Picasso); M. Pichon, Mme Demagny (musée Rodin); M. Viton, Mme Poubeau (préfecture de Région Île-de-France); M. Feyfant (Régie immobilière de la Ville de Paris); M. Longuet Guyon des Diguères (ministère de l'Économie, des Finances et de l'Industrie); M. de Corta, M. Franque (Service d'information des relations publiques de l'armée); M. Chierici (Sogetim); M. Lescure (Ville de Paris); Mme Monié.

PHOTO CREDITS

In the same series

CITIES OF ART

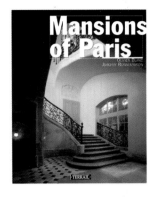

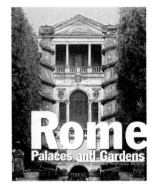

ARCHITECTURE

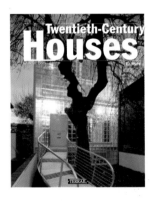

ANCIENT CIVILIZATIONS

- The Ancient Near East
- The Pharaohs Master-Builders
- The Gold of the Pharaohs
- Art of Ancient Greece
- Pompeii

PRIMITIVE ARTS

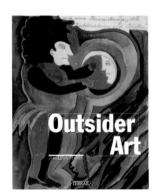

- Black Africa
- Art and Craft in Africa
- Native Arts of North America

PAINTING / SCULPTURE

- Outsider Art
- Duchamp & Co.
- Picasso
- Paris-Montparnasse
- Paris-Montmartre
- Kandinsky
- Modigliani
- The Fauves
- Gauguin and the Nabis
- Rodin
- Mucha
- Caspar David Friedrich
- Masters of English Landscape
- Michelangelo
- Leonardo
- Early Flemish Painting

·TERRAIL·